THE STREETS OF
PARIS

THE STREETS OF PARIS

Introduction and text by

RICHARD COBB

Photographs by

NICHOLAS BREACH

Pantheon Books, New York

All rights reserved under International and Pan-American Copyright Conventions. Published in the United States by Pantheon Books, a division of Random House, Inc., New York. Originally published in Great Britain by Gerald Duckworth & Co., Ltd.

LIBRARY OF CONGRESS CATALOGING IN PUBLICATION DATA

Cobb, Richard Charles, 1917–
The streets of Paris.

1. Paris—Description—1975–   —Views.
I. Breach, Nicholas. II. Title.
DC707.C6   944′.361   79-3574
ISBN 0-394-51026-7
ISBN 0-394-73865-9 pbk.

Manufactured in the United States of America

FIRST AMERICAN EDITION

CONTENTS

*To my friend Bill Fishman,
another walking historian,
in the hope that he will
enjoy these walks in Paris
as much as I have enjoyed
walking with him in his
beloved East End.*

. . . D'où que tu es?
De Tancarville près du Havre.
Moua chsui dparis, dit Thérèse
Des Cigales retira gravement la pipe de son bec. Il dit
De Paris emprès Pontoise.
J'ai été une fois au Havre, dit Thérèse, voir la
mer et les paquebots. C'est curieux . . .
RAYMOND QUENEAU, *Loin de Rueil,* 1944

INTRODUCTION

PARIS IS A manageable place; its frontiers are clearly marked, there is no doubt as to where it begins and where it ends, though, porte des Lilas, porte de Montreuil, porte de Versailles, there is a fairly wide intermediate zone. It is above all manageable physically, in that it can be walked from end to end, east to west, Vincennes to Neuilly; from north to south, Clignancourt to Orléans, though I have never in fact done either in one go. I have, however, walked through the night from Viroflay to Odéon, passing the longest DEFENSE D'AFFICHER I have ever encountered, the apparently interminable wall of the Renault car factory in Billancourt; and, at regular intervals, between one and three in the morning, the whole length of the rue de Vaugirard whether from Issy-les-Moulineaux or the Lycée Michelet, in Vanves, past *Convention* and *boutons et jours*, to the corner of the rue de Tournon facing the Senate. Other nights have taken me from the centre of Montrouge again to the rue de Tournon. I have come down from the top of the rue de Ménilmontant, through the rue Oberkampf, and past the *Café du Centenaire* (which no longer exists, as if the memory of 1789 had been officially erased, the café now being replaced by a Wimpy Bar) and down through the Gravilliers, again to the rue de Tournon. Having fallen asleep in the *métro*, at the *Nation* terminus, when I eventually woke up, I found myself in complete darkness, at the end of a tunnel. Having reached the platform, I was finally able to find my way up a fire-escape, making my way home, a little before dawn, down the whole dreary length of the boulevard Voltaire; and the walk from the rue d'Argentine (ex-Obligado) to the VIme was a more regular nightly occurrence. Whether from choice or necessity—no money for a ticket, or the last *métro* gone—there are very few Paris itineraries that, at one time or another, I have *not* had to walk. This has stood me in good stead, for Paris *should* be walked, because much of it, the most secret, the most modest, the most bizarre, the tiniest, is only discoverable by the pedestrian who is prepared to push behind the boulevards and the long straight streets of the Second Empire and the early confident years of the Third Republic. It is as if a different city, made up of tiny courtyards and diminutive houses, were prepared to reveal its unpretentious and endearing proportions only to the walker, still clinging to early-nineteenth-century forms of transport and the itineraries imposed by the amount that two legs can tackle. Certainly cars have—should have—no place either in the impasse Coeur de Vey (XIVme) or in the passage Dieu (XXme), and only the owners and workers of the *Etablissements Dupont*, the makers of luxury cigarette-lighters, are likely to have been aware of the existence of the tiny rue Dieu (Xme). The numerous *passages* of the quartier Saint-Lazare, the quartier de la Bourse, off the rue Mazagran, and other parts of central Paris can only be negotiated on foot. Aragon wrote *Le Paysan de Paris*, while still a young man, with his feet. Most of this sort of Paris is invisible to those too who rely on public transport (though the *métro aérien*, between *Nationale* and *Glacière*, between *la Motte-Picquet* and *Bir Hakiem* or in some of its northern loops above *la Chapelle* may offer many suggestive, tempting, if fleeting views of third- and fourth-floor interiors: bedrooms, kitchens, figures silhouetted at night against drawn blinds, while the vast cutaways at the approaches to the Gare du Nord and Saint-Lazare present a whole range of windows, some with washing, windows that are only discoverable from the line) because so much of the city is closed off in courtyards, down alley-ways, or beyond narrow *entrées*. A great deal of the city is still, as it was in the eighteenth century, an enfilade of tall green *portes cochères*, ornamented with heavy brass knockers, lions' heads, their golden tongues hanging out; and even now it is a place that secretes hundreds of hidden gardens, the foliage of which is sometimes visible from the street, peering over a wall, but many of which may be spied only once in a lifetime, thanks to the chance opening of an eighteenth-century double-door, approached by two sets of curling steps—*le perron—côté cour,* in a former *hôtel particulier.* For twenty years I lived in a room facing onto the courtyard of 12 rue de Tournon, a house built in 1778, and only once did I get a clear view of the tiny garden that lay beyond the main ground-floor apartment. Of course I was never able actually to set foot in it, so that it acquired the great desirability of inaccessibility and mystery, like the garden of a convent.

It is what lies *beyond* the *porte cochère,* or past the narrow entry into a deep rectangular courtyard that is so often the most rewarding, and the most unexpected. *Escalier D, au fond de la Cour, fabrique de banjos, Escalier J, au fond de la Cour à gauche, mécanicien* as well as providing a necessary indication to the complication of Parisian addresses in these enclosed places that can still be described as survivals of eighteenth-century *Cours des Miracles,* especially in the older central, east-central, and north-eastern districts (Hébert's newspaper, *le Père Duchesne,* lay in the Cour de la rue Neuve-l'Egalité, a courtyard which still exists off what is now—conquest having come in between—la rue d'Aboukir), should be taken as a slogan, and as an invitation, as challenging as an unexpected *fonds d'archives* is to the historian, to anyone who wants to get to know the city and to push beyond the formal façades of the *grands boulevards* triumphal arches and the geometrical perspectives of streets, arcades and buildings designed for collective show and for the glorification of State power. *Les Mystères de Paris* lurk in dank, leprous places, and Haussmann knew what he was doing when he ordered the levelling of the Butte-des-Moulins to make way for the avenue de l'Opéra, and cut through the maze of the old *cité,* rue de Jérusalem, the lair of the *tapis francs,* to construct, in their place, an enormous neo-gothic Palais de Justice, the triumph of Authority over Individualism. At least that is how I see it, that is the angle of vision that gives me most satisfaction. Just as I like my history to look inwards, from light into semi-darkness, from the street into the interior, if possible even to cross the threshold and negotiate the dark staircase, enjoying on the hand the smooth curling wood of the banister, just as I want my historical itineraries to be capable of reconstruction in terms of both walking distance and regular habit—to and from work, the different itineraries of leisure or of the seasons, and again the different *promenades de dimanche*—all of which will contribute to a

sense of reassurance, because of predictability and continuity (because *dis*continuity in history is utterly alarming), so I feel that Paris should be both walkable and walked, if the limitless variety, the unexpectedness, the provincialism, the rusticity, the touching eccentricity, and the often tiny scale of the place are to be appreciated.

Of course, Paris, like any big city, represents a very large number of choices, ranging from the show spots, the garish quarters of vice and pleasure, to the stuffy, selfish, self-satisfied wastes of the Avenue Henri-Martin. Most have something to offer, including the churches and the historic buildings. But the Paris I prefer is that of the minute, intimate, or semi-intimate domestic scale, not that of the village—for there cannot be a village in the absence of a church, and churches I have excluded, as I have other historic edifices—but at least a couple of streets, whether dormant and semi-rural, or busy with small shops and barrows, cafés, and people carrying black shopping bags. Generally it is not very hard for the man on foot to discover, though he needs to step behind the scenes, behind those stern and unremitting friezes of tall uniform houses, drilled to Haussmann specifications, six or seven storeys, *chambres mansardées* at the top to accommodate the maids, bulbous, tummied balconies, sometimes supported by allegorical beasts or female sphinxes wearing breast-plates and terminating halfway down, in sad grey stone or yellowish brick—Second Empire, Third Republic, or late-1920-style H. B. M. in yellow with green or blue lozenge motifs—the jumble of small houses, sheds, workshops, *impasses, passages,* former stables, of only two or three storeys, as if shy of visitors, and anxious to conceal their still rural proportions, their peeling plaster, the fading advertisements on their cut-off sides, or the still just visible lettering of a trade or of an inviting restaurant or café-title, their unassuming traces of care and intimacy: cages of canaries, potted plants, hanging up outside at head level, the communal tap in the form of an iron dolphin, dilapidated shutters, a profusion of chimneys and stove-pipes, the wiring and the pipes, shivering and gurgling, and both appearing highly dangerous, curling like jungle vegetation—stifling green *lianes* of suppurating sweat—around entry walls and up dim staircases, as if living off the damp stone and attempting to strangle the building and its tenants, a cluster of letter-boxes, double-surnamed (husband and wife), some in spidery handwriting, some with printed visiting cards and *titres* (even little crosses for the *Légion,* palms, lyres, and so on) the complicated plans at the entrance to the *loge* representing the names and locations of the various *locataires,* and the entries to staircases which run through the first part of the alphabet, *Escalier A, Escalier K* (I have even seen an *Escalier M,* but an *Escalier W* has eluded me).

This book then depicts, in visual terms that are as minute as technique will allow, a Paris that is both half-hidden, and, because it is unpretentious and takes up a great deal of space with its low-lying buildings and long yards, increasingly threatened. I make no apology for the multiplicity of pictures of courtyards, for I think that they offer one of the most abiding charms of the city; they also condition the friendly sociability of their inhabitants, the washing lines shared, the children watched from a score of inward-looking windows and stairways, their pets roaming at will, a stream of soapy water running through the central channel (*rigole*) of the paved yard. With almost the sole exception of the rue du Faubourg Saint-Martin—one of the oldest streets in Paris, and, until Haussmann, with its twin, the rue du Faubourg Saint-Denis, the principal north-south axis of the city—I have had no difficulty in avoiding the main arteries and the wide boulevards, choosing, on the contrary, side streets that are still paved and down which will run streams of water, at the bid of the long brooms of uniformed municipal employees concerned with *la voierie.* On such streets, as well as on busier ones such as the rue de Ménilmontant, the intention has been to take in at least one example of every common trade and of every type of small shop: *couleurs* (they smell nice and they are pretty), *vins, alimentation, vins-charbons, coiffure, laverie, blanchisserie-pressing, fumisterie, coutellerie, serrurerie, boulangerie-pâtisserie, enseignes, papeterie, électricité, mercerie, boutons et jours, cordonnerie, boucherie, médailles et décorations, tailleur, imprimerie, mécanique, tôlerie, chauffage, ambulances, doreur, relieur, remaillage, tampons, jouets, farces et attrapes, postiches, ceintures, soutiens-gorge, gaines, vieux papiers, bouchons, métaux et chiffons,* small workshops, cafés, bars, restaurants. The only trade that managed to elude us was that of the *pompes funèbres,* death having long since escaped from the modest proportions of the small shop; and, despite much study of the names in the *loges* of *concierges,* we were unable to discover a single *Madame Irma,* fakir, or *cartomancienne.* Perhaps we should have looked in the XIIme.

In short, a place of human proportions and in which most people can give names and greetings to most people, in which a couple of men, or a couple of women, will linger, holding their black *cabas,* with leeks and carrots sticking out of them, to exchange a few words, after making a purchase, in which there is time to linger, and in which the shopkeeper, behind his counter, will take a professional pride in his ability to hold the attention of the prospective customer:

> Bonjour, madame, beau temps, n'est-ce pas? Dame! voilà bientôt l'été. Pour une miniature ou pour une photographie? Photographie. Et quel format? Vous ne le savez paz? L'avez-vous avec vous, cette photo? Non? Alors, chère madame, comment voulez-vous que je vous vende un cadre? Vous voulez le choisir, comme ça? Au jugé? Quelle grave erreur, madame ... Je ne fais pas du travail d'amateur ... Ce serait un crime de mettre dans n'importe quoi l'image d'un être cher ... Votre fils? Vous voyez ... Treize ans? Et il sait déjà ce qu'il veut faire? Ah! ingénieur. C'est un beau métier ...

Queneau's photographer has all the time in the world, as well as a remarkable *baratin.* The sales talk is as important as the sale. This is not the sort of Paris in which impatient people will rush blindly from or into a *bouche de métro,* their eyes turned inwards, on the unseeing journey to work or back home. On the contrary, it is a leisured place, walkable in all its limits, and in which there is the opportunity to dawdle, to stop, to see, to notice small changes and to have one's attention caught by a drawn blind, by a closed shutter, by a shop-door without its handle, by the small square of a white notice, *fermé pour cause de décès,* or *fermé jusqu' au Ier septembre,* by a sign-painter painting out a familiar name, by a child's face at a window, by a geranium in flower.

Two of the areas included, the Xme and the XXme, represented, in the roundabout itinerary covered on foot, the passing of a complete day, at least during the hours of October light, from 7-ish to 6.30, so that it might be possible to follow the activities of a quarter and the movements of its inhabitants through the day and at least from hour to hour, and preferably from a fixed and unobtrusive vantage point. In the Xme, the footbridge over the canal offered us, over several hours, the view from the captain's bridge, both waterwards and quayside-wards, and even beyond the quays, towards the interior. In the XXme, we did a full circle, ending up much where we had started from, rue des Amandiers. In both *arrondissements,* by the end of the time, we had

9

begun recognising people, and begun being recognised by them.

The two of us, the tripod and the photographic equipment, one of us ahead and scouting out courtyards and *entrées,* the names on *loges,* objects in windows, the other following on, burdened with a clutter of equipment, had become part of the familiar landscape. In these two areas of north-east Paris, at least, we were able to perceive what Jules Romains, in *le 6 octobre,* has called *la respiration de la grande ville,* a living entity breathing through the hours of the day and the coming night. The other areas were covered over shorter periods of time, though we often stopped long enough to see the people who had gone in (a shop, a café, a restaurant, a park) coming out. We chose weekdays because we wanted a landscape with people, wanted too to be able to distinguish between a Wednesday and a Thursday, between mid-week and a Friday (when people have more money to spend); and so we avoided the unusual movements of a Saturday, or the Sunday stillness save in the neighbourhood of cemeteries. And we chose early October, not in deference to *le 6 octobre* (itself, however, an excellent choice, just after *la rentrée,* with everyone back in the city and oysters on the stalls, a pre-1914 Thursday), but because the October light of the Ile-de-France seemed especially favourable to what we had in mind. There would have been little point in operating in the dead month of August, *la morte saison* indeed, rows of closed shops, their shutters down; and winter would have been too uncomfortable for work carried out mainly outside, though occasionally under the cover of a glass roof, or a balcony, or in the entry of a staircase. We took a risk on the weather and were lucky. But then October is nearly always the best month in Paris; and those who have been away are glad to be back in the city—perhaps the only justification, as far as I can see, for the almost professional zeal that the French—the most stylised, elaborately dressed, eleborately equipped *vacanciers,* a nation in fact of Hulots, of any Europeans—devote to the serious, elaborate and tiresome business of summer holidays. In October, these at least are over, the *bronzage* has been completed, and everything is open again.

The responsibility for the *arrondissements* in part covered, and, more important, for those left out, lies entirely with the author. They represent in fact hardly a tenth of the total area of the city; and a similar topography, whether squat and low-lying, or climbing steeply northwards, and as friendly and as provincial,

could certainly have been illustrated elsewhere: for instance in the adjoining XIXme, as much part of Belleville-Ménilmontant as the XXme—indeed, we strayed into it on more than one occasion, and as much part of Dabit's Paris of the 20s and 30s as the Xme and the XVIIIme; or in the quartier des Ternes, in and around the rue des Acacias and in the *Villas* beyond the church of Saint-Ferdinand; or in the *Village Suisse,* near la Motte-Piquet-Grenelle, off the rue de Siam; or in and off the rue Saint-Charles; or in the rue des Favorites and the coaching-inns and former stables near the *Centre des Comptes-Chèques-Postaux* in the XVme; even in some shopping streets in les Batignolles, just off the boulevard Malesherbes; or in the hidden wastes and narrow streets off the boulevard de Picpus, in the XIIme. This is merely a selection, and one which will perhaps tempt others to look further, at least on the Right Bank.

The XVIme, the VIIIme, and most of the central areas excluded themselves. The old Halles is a sad desert; the Marais has become a museum, its original inhabitants dispersed to the *grande banlieue,* and replaced by middle-class intellectuals, their wives dressed like Gipsey-Rose-Lees in expensive rags, and armed with *le Nouvel-Observateur,* or by young technocratic couples, fresh from the *Grandes Ecoles* or from the provinces. The quartier Saint-Merri has been frozen into a network of *voies piétonnes,* one of the surest ways of congealing a once-living quarter into the slow death of fashion, tourism, sex-shops, antique-shops and expensive *boutiques;* in the rue Quincampoix, the small cafés have given way to bars and couscous restaurants. The Ile-Saint-Louis is for millionaires, its central street for picture-galleries. The Gravilliers and the Temple have indeed survived, but they have never had any large concentrations of nineteenth-century domestic architecture. The VIme has been lost beyond hope—the last hope was the old marché Saint-Germain; the *librairie* Clavreuil, in the rue Saint-André-des-Arts the only shop left of the street as it was in the 1930s, a last outpost of a once living quarter, quartier de Buci: *on est entouré d'étrangers,* comments sadly Clavreuil fils; the VIIme is similarly infected, the quartier Saint-Séverin is totally ruined.

I feel sentimental about the Xme because, like Louis Chevalier, who began to discover Paris in the company of the son of a *concierge,* boulevard Sébastopol, I began there, quartier Bonne-Nouvelle, in sight of *le Rex, le Matin,* and the rue de la Lune, in 1935, my own *apprentissage de Paris* (and I could hardly have had a more Parisian apprenticeship, save in the XXme or the XIXme). But the Xme, especially in its eastern and north-eastern quarters, is also largely unspoilt and little known, once one leaves the *grands boulevards* and the two triumphal arches of the Porte Saint-Denis and the Porte Saint-Martin, for so long the official point of entry of victorious armies, not always French, and so part of public history and topography. The XXme was chosen because it is like no other quarter—save parts of the adjoining XIXme, likewise steep, and likewise sharing parts of Belleville—and because it is well aware of its uniquely cosmopolitan and popular identity. A great many people—from Dabit onwards—have written about *les gas de Belleville*, none better than Louis Chevalier in his *les Parisiens*, but none, so far as I know, has illustrated this high citadel of *l'esprit parisien* (which, in the nineteenth century, emigrated northwards and up the hill, abandoning the rue Saint-Denis, described as the quintessence of Parisian cheek and Parisian irreverence by Mercier and Restif in the previous century). Since then, too, it has remained a citadel of mutual tolerance as between fellow Bellevillois and Bellevilloises, taking in wave after wave of immigration, first from the Massif Central and the Midi, then from the Jewish *stetl'* of Central and Eastern Europe, more recently, Algerians, Senegalese, Guinéens, Gabonais, much of francophone West Africa, so that, rue Ramponeau, a poster in Arabic script advertising an Egyptian film will lie side by side with a poster in Hebrew script announcing a religious festival (this is after all the terrain of Emile Ajar, of the childhood of a very alert boy, *la vie devant soi*). So the inclusion of Belleville-Ménilmontant needs no justification, the pictures of the up-and-down place speak eloquently for themselves. The XVIIIme tempted me by the sheer beauty of the name of the quarter, *la Goutte-d'Or*, and by the sinister reputation it acquired as a daily and nightly killing ground during the Algerian War. I wanted at last to explore the *casbah*; but I found much more than I had counted for: rural islands, a *Villa*, sunny houses discovered up steep steps. For a year or more I gave English lessons to an Egyptian film producer—he made very bad films for the Cairo market—who lived above the cutting in the rue Geoffroy Saint-Hilaire, almost opposite Jussieu's cedar on its *butte*, and who used to take me to drink mint tea at the Mosque, so I came to appreciate the area of the Vme that extended from the rue Poliveau to the rue des Boulangers; and for several years I had eaten *chez Mimile*, above the place Lucien-Herr. Much of this part

of the Vme has survived, though with many gaps, like bad teeth. Finally, the quartier de Gergovie, the only interesting area in the otherwise sadly banal and often rather mean and hopeless—what could be more wretched than the rue Gassendi—XIVme, seemed to call out pathetically for attention, before its small houses and amazing courtyards were smothered by the spreading horror of Maine-Montparnasse.

Each picture has a story to tell; whether the story it tells is the story that I have attempted to make it tell is a matter of opinion. Some may think I have tried to read too much into what would seem to them a portrait of complete predictability and banality, or that I have been at pains to point out the obvious, or even that I have been too free with the pedagogic pointers: 'note this', 'note that'. Readers may think that I have over-indulged a personal taste for detail, for minutiae, a concern for objects, merely because they have come—or will come—in contact with human beings. Anyhow, they will soon form their own opinion as to that; they can always skip the commentary, and treat this merely as a picture book, and a very beautiful one at that.

For it is the result of close collaboration between two friends. As Nicholas Breach and I walked immense distances around Paris, he loaded with heavy equipment, I, my hands free, running ahead, pegging out claims, here to a courtyard, there to a menu, to a banister, to a cluster of colour, we soon developed a visual unity that enabled us to use two pairs of eyes as one. Each shot is the result of our mutual reaction to a building, a crimson bedspread, a face, a piece of faded lettering; we responded similarly and simultaneously to a shaft of sunlight on a grey peeling wall, to the bright colours of fruit, to the faded blues of an old restaurant sign; and, once we had begun together, Nicholas could certainly have gone on alone. I like to think, however, that, each day, our understanding grew, that we became both surer of foot and surer of eye. Nicholas never complained when I put before him yet another courtyard, another *entrée*, another dark stairway curling upwards, and I believe that I soon made of him a convert to my own obsession with minutiae. It is for this reason that, with a single exception (the second photograph of the *Villa Poissonnière*) I have retained the exact order in which we walked our daily collaboration, starting with the XIVme, then the Vme, then a day in Belleville-Ménilmontant, the XXme, one day in the Xme, ending with the XVIIIme. As we did an awful lot of walking, so let others walk with us, but perhaps at a more leisurely pace, so anxious were we to use the maximum of the October light. I say this as much out of respect for our ill-used feet (though, at the end of the day, in the Xme, they were offered, in promise at least, the balm of pedicure) as for a mutual understanding that grew hour by hour. I knew from the start what I wanted; but I had no idea how to get it. Nicholas was the magician who made this, I find, beautiful, collection of photographs possible. There was nothing that I asked him to do that he could not do, even to the extent of showing the details of every name in a *loge de concierge*, 3 rue Vercingétorix, or of going in uncommercial pursuit of a prostitute, already on the beat at 8 a.m., boulevard de la Chapelle.

Titles always present problems. I had thought of *Villages of Paris*; but then these are not villages. To call the collection *Disappearing Paris* would be both a misnomer and an expression of undue pessimism. There may be a nostalgic tone about much of the comments; I do not like what is happening to Paris, and I greatly prefer the Paris of the 1930s or of the 1950s to the Paris of the 1970s. But, in fact, this book is an effort at reassurance, and I have indeed managed to reassure myself (partly by taking care to avoid the VIme and similar ruined quarters). I think much will still be standing when the book appears. I was then briefly tempted by a title that at least had the merit of being literal: *A Pedestrian's Paris*, for that is what it was; nor could it have been discovered in any other way; but it also *sounded* pedestrian! So I finally opted for *The Streets of Paris*, taken to include what so often leads off them. And few street-walkers—the professionals generally being assigned to a very limited, acknowledged beat (*la rade*)—can have covered quite so much distance in so short a time.

What added to our excitement and, despite fatigue, our enjoyment, was the friendly curiosity of everyone we met, in the course of our prospections. They told us about the sins of landlords and landladies, the threats of expulsion or demolition, the wickedness of architects and of planners; they allowed us into their staircases, and seemed actually pleased when we took shots of their washing. Why were we doing it? Surely this old building was not worth recording? Would we send them the photograph, when printed? There was only one occasion when we were forced to retreat from a courtyard that had seemed promising, only one other when we were greeted by a storm of very Parisian abuse. Our book, which is mostly about *le petit peuple*, while in the making gave us daily examples of the *gentillesse* and the humour of *le petit peuple*. No one accused us of slumming; and we were welcomed into courtyard after courtyard, as if we had every right to be there. Naturally, children were particularly interested in us, and particularly insistent that they should be in our book, so we had to put them in, as much to please them as to add lightness and joy to our account.

In historical research, there are two stages of sheer enjoyment: the one, the actual collection of the material, the physical presence of boxes of eighteenth-century *procès-verbaux*, the dirt of a hundred and eighty years on one's hands, the excitement of recognition or of repetition, the gradual realisation that one is watching the unfolding of a very complex and exciting human story, the illustration of banality, the revelation of the inventiveness of popular humour, the satisfied acquisitiveness of the collector; the other, the writing-up, the mulling over each document, the discovery of details previously unnoticed, even the emergence of some vaguely perceived pattern. It is exactly this double pleasure that I have felt, first while walking with Nicholas, collecting our evidence, then, much later—for I have dawdled even more than usual, when putting it all together. This book has been great fun to write; I hope it will be fun to read.

Wolvercote   R.C.C.

I

XIVme arrondissement:
quartier de Gergovie and quartier de l'Ouest.

. . . Sur la porte, une pancarte: *Mme Saphir. Passé. Présent. Avenir. On entre si la serrure n'est pas fermée à clef. On prend son Numéro Magique sur la table et l'on attend d'être appelé par le nombre de coups de sonnette correspondant au dit Numéro. Tarifs humanitaires* . . . Il descendit l'escalier sans avoir rencontré personne . . . traversa la cour du 12 . . . reprit le passage, puis le long boyau qui longeait le chantier de bois, referma une porte à clé.

Ayant ainsi savouré les mystères de Paris, il se retrouva chez lui . . .

RAYMOND QUENEAU, *Le dimanche de la vie*, 1951

'. . . Le logement se composait d'une seule pièce qu'encombraient deux lits, des chaises, une armoire à glace, une table, une cuisinière . . . Cirer l'escalier "du devant", laver l'escalier "du fond", balayer la cour, astiquer les cuivres, s'occuper du courrier, des receveurs de la compagnie du gaz; enfin, tous les trois mois, toucher le terme. Quel souci, alors!'

EUGÈNE DABIT, *Faubourgs de Paris*, 1933

THE TWO quarters are just off the Avenue du Maine, and south of the quartier de la Gaîté, the one-time terrain of Charles-Louis Philippe's *Bubu de Montparnasse*. It is an area in visible decline, once inhabited by Breton immigrants, and now partly given over to the Algerians and Portuguese. The quarter is limited to the west by the main line out of the new Gare du Maine, at one time dominated by a plaster lion with a curly tail that stared out at the trains from a wall adjoining a *crêperie bretonne*; but the whole street has now gone, and the deep courtyards of the rue de l'Ouest and the rue Vercingétorix seem similarly threatened. However, a mixed population of artists, sculptors and painters managed to hold on, in the small streets off the rue Raymond Losserand, the rest of the quarter is inhabited by small tradesmen; artisans and *retraités* (particularly rue des Postes). Most of the cafés are run by Bretons, most of the prostitutes, rue Sauvageot, off the rue de l'Ouest, are still Bretonnes. The quarter developed mainly during the 1840s and 1850s, provoked no doubt in part by the construction of the *chemin-de-fer de l'Ouest*. Further to the south, nearer the *ceinture*, there are small market-gardens, and in the rue Brancion (XVme), large men in bloody leather jackets reaching their feet slaughter horses, day and night, Opposite the slaughterhouse, there is a *boucherie chevaline* with thirteen golden horses' heads. The area is predominantly petit-bourgeois with a population older than in any *arrondissement* other than that of the Vme. But the resident population is threatened by the further development of the Maine-Montparnasse tower blocks, which is likewise erasing the rural character of much of Gergovie. However, more has survived here than on the other side of the main line, in the XVme, around the old coaching inns of the rue des Favorites. This part of the XIVme has no particular historical links. Lenin lived in the other end of the *arrondissement*, the far side of the avenue d'Orléans, in the ultra-respectable, yellow-bricked rue Marie-Rose. Further still, the quarter of the Cité Universitaire houses a large proportion of University professors and *lycée* teachers. But middle-class professional people are beginning to encamp on the fringes of Gergovie, which, as well as being an area traditionally given up to the aged, is also peopled by the very young, owing to the *maternité Plaisance*, rue Legouis. In the 1950s, the rue de l'Ouest was one of the most drunken streets in Paris.

1 Boulangerie-Pâtisserie, 124 rue du Chateau, XIVme.

A corner shop, with Second Empire coloured panels, quartier de Gergovie. Rousseau, in *Les Confessions*, described his pleasure at gazing into the windows of a *boulangerie*, picking out the fresh-faced girls in white aprons. This is the sort of shop to be visited on a Sunday morning, after church, to pick up presents, wrapped up and tied with golden string, for one's hosts at lunch. Here it is early in the morning with customers waiting to buy *baguettes*.

2 General view of courtyard, 9 rue de l'Ouest, XIVme.

The rue de l'Ouest is well-named, as it is alongside the mainline to Brest, the old *Etat*. The quartier de Gergovie in which it is situated, just beyond the quartier de la Gaîté, is less so; for Vercingétorix does not belong to a quarter mostly inhabited by Bretons and in which there are few Auvergnats. A bearded carpenter in blues, whose workshop is at the far end of the courtyard, told us that the buildings were threatened with demolition, the landlady allowing them to fall into a state of disrepair, so as to be able to obtain a demolition order. In the vicinity the huge mass of Maine-Montparnasse seems to underline the threat to the mainly Louis-Philippe quarter of hidden yards and small studios, so this may well be a last view of what was till recently an artisanal environment.

3 9 rue de l'Ouest, XIVme.
Another view of the threatened courtyard, showing
the entry onto the street. A contented cat is sitting at
the window on the right. The room over the archway
has a half-drawn curtain in red and white check.

RIGHT
4 Tap in courtyard, 9 rue de l'Ouest, XIVme.
A fine piece of nineteenth-century ironwork
decorating the communal tap, with dish-cloths drying
on the railings behind.

FAR RIGHT
5 Far end of courtyard, 9 rue de l'Ouest, XIVme.
Escalier E (the courtyard advances quite a long way
through the alphabet) at the far end, with the
carpenter's workshop, and an ivy-strewn house with a
pretty red roof recently repaired, as though there
might still be hope of a reprieve for the jumble of
buildings grouped around the deep courtyard.

**6   House at far end of courtyard, 9 rue de
l'Ouest, XIVme.**
Another house, in advanced disrepair, but just alive,
as though winking through one open window, the two
oeil-de-boeuf giving the façade rather a southern
appearance, though the house on the left is
reassuringly Ile-de-France. *Escalier F* is on the right.

7   Entry to Escalier D, courtyard of 9 rue de l'Ouest, XIVme.
Escalier D is very domesticated, giving witness to care: plants on a shelf, a bright coloured bird in a cage, washing on the line at two levels, all seem to defy the bulldozer.

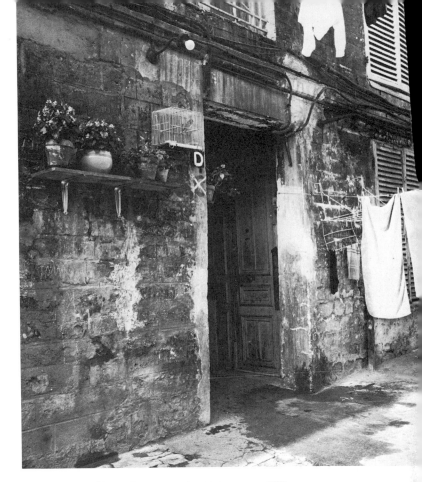

8   17 rue Perrel opposite the rue Vercingétorix
The street comes to a sudden end just beyond the house on the left. Looking down it, one can see the expresses from or to the West of France passing a little above the level of the small street, most of which has already been demolished. The two houses facing south still show signs of life; but the bulldozers are already at work, making way for more Maine-Montparnasses. The street itself has been deprived of its blue and white *plaque* which was no doubt on the corner house where there is a space to the right.

LEFT ABOVE

9 Shopfront, 4 rue Perrel, opposite 65 rue Vercingétorix, XIVme.
The shop, a rich bottle-green, looks depressingly closed, as though the handle had not been placed in the door for many months. Yet it has been freshly painted and the upper windows are open.

LEFT BELOW

10 Shopfront, 65 rue Vercingétorix, XIVme.
Another small 1830–40 shop-front, dark red (*lie de vin*), also very shut and hopeless, protecting its emptiness with a flowered veil, as though after death. No. 65 looks onto the doomed street cut off by the railway embankment.

11 Hôtel de l'Industrie, 65 rue Vercingétorix, XIVme.
The very faint and peeling reminder, in Second Empire lettering, *Chambres au mois, Chambres à la journée* at each end, of the past social history of the quartier de Gergovie, the home of immigrant Breton workers, settling near the old Gare du Montparnasse, most of them building labourers. *L'Industrie* must have spelt moral qualities; for there never has been any industry in this part of Paris. The hotel looks like a nineteenth-century *garni* for single men. There are traces of shutters on the peeling walls. The lettering is pale yellow on faded red.

21

12 The courtyard of an abandoned school, rue Vercingétorix, XIVme.
Now used as a social centre for Portuguese immigrant workers and their families. The two children at play could speak no French and had very large dark eyes.

13 Courtyard, 55 rue Vercingétorix, XIVme.
An abandoned *pissotière* and two houses inhabited by Portuguese immigrant workers who have taken the place of the Bretons.

14 53 rue Vercingétorix, XIVme.
The peeling wall is like a painter's
palette: faded yellows, a flaking red,
strips of blue; the drinkers have gone,
the one-time café-bar has an air of
complete hopelessness, *Suffren*, as a
telephone exchange, has long since
been overtaken, along with *Danton,
Odéon, Jasmin, Nord, Botzaris,
Daumesnil*, by computerised numbers.

15 Rue Vercingétorix, XIVme.
A small factory, Second Empire or
Third Republic, off the street, and
out of keeping with surroundings
mainly artisanal.

16   3 rue Vercingétorix, XIVme.
A very long courtyard, near the beginning of the street
and almost in the shadow of Maine-Montparnasse,
with intense building activity in the street just
beyond. An Algerian face could be seen staring rather
listlessly through the foliage almost covering the
window on the north side of the courtyard. The
entrance to *Escalier G* is below the cluster of clothes.

17   Courtyard, 3 rue Vercingétorix, XIVme.
The east side of the same courtyard, a workshop on
the far left of a *sculpteur-marbrier* containing, gleaming
in the semi-darkness, some fifty busts of Homer and as
many of Dante, seated among which is the bearded
sculptor himself, an elderly Italian, the first floor
inhabited by an Algerian family.

18   Courtyard, 3 rue Vercingétorix, XIVme.
The south view of the courtyard, the front door of a
converted workshop approached by a piece of squared
washable matting retrieved from a bathroom or a
kitchen, the door itself protected by a Mediterranean
curtain in green plastic strips, each indicating modest
efforts at domesticity; the shutters have been
recovered from another part of the rambling building.

**19   Loge de concierge, courtyard, 3 rue
Vercingétorix, XIVme.**
The full plan of the *Cour des Miracles*, staircase by
staircase, the ground-floor on the left, with several
workshops: *papeterie parisienne, coiffeur, capelier* (sic),
électricien plombier, porcelainier, café françois, Escaliers
A, B, C, D, E, F, G, H, I, J, two de la Morinerie, a
series of names, mostly French; on the right, first and

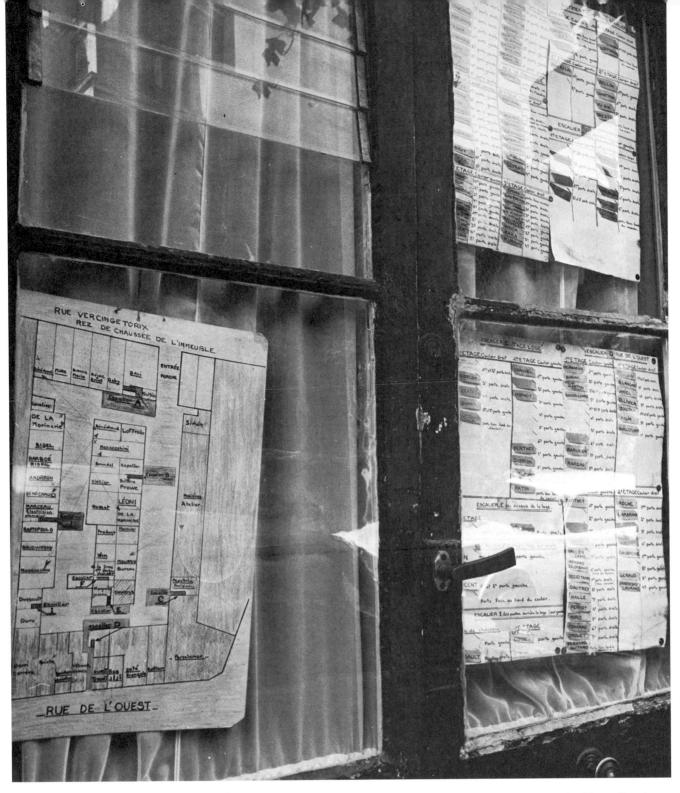

second storeys, by staircase, names attached, mostly French; top right, third storey, more names, some of them exotic. A plan as elaborate as that of Bourges cathedral, and eloquent of the crowded jumble of courtyard neighbourliness. The *loge* is firmly shut and locked, the handle of the door removed against enquiries, it is up to the visitor to find his way among the Murrays, the Wodas, the Miros, the Dalis, the Léonis, the Guinios, the Janowkys, the Zoccolis, the Vieux-Jeantons, the Karas, the Evénos, the Efredos, the Vugias, the Salvador Perreiras, the Pelikans, the Krieffs, and, on the ground floor, Bob Jiji.

20 Courtyard, 3 rue Vercingétorix
With a few more inhabitants, not listed on the windows
of the *loge*, but equally well established.

2

Vme arrondissement:

quartier du Jardin des Plantes and quartier Mouffetard.

'. . . Il est cordonnier Jacques l'Aumône. Il a maintenant 70 ans. Il se tient dans son échoppe depuis 50 ans. Il n'en bouge pas. Il ne sort jamais de Paris. Le dimanche il travaille jusqu' à midi, puis il s'assoit sur un banc . . . Il ne s'est pas marié. Il n'a pas de parents ni d'amis. Il se fait lui-même sa cuisine. Il mange peu . . . il ne baise pas . . .'

RAYMOND QUENEAU, *Loin de Rueil*, 1944

ACCORDING TO Louis Chevalier, writing in the 1960s, and an inhabitant of the quarter, the Vme contains a larger proportion of people over 60, with a preponderance of women: retired shop-keepers, *employées*, than any other area of the city. Certainly, to judge from the regular visitors to the Jardin des Plantes, there would seem to be no lack of elderly people of both sexes in the area. The quartier Mouffetard was for several centuries a stronghold of *le petit commerce*; but the street and the surrounding area have changed profoundly in the last ten years, with the discovery of their tourist attractions and with the destruction of several sections of the rue Mouffetard itself, a process begun in the 1930s and that resulted in 1935 in the discovery of a hoard of Louis XIV gold pieces, the *trésor de la rue Mouffetard*. The eastern side of the *arrondissement*, based on the spine of the rue Geoffroy Saint-Hilaire, has been less affected by such developments than the western, in dangerous proximity to the hideous Boulevard Saint-Michel and the quartier des Ecoles. But there are still pockets of unassuming peace and habit in the rue Lhomond and the rue de l'Arbre-sec, thanks in part to the extent of ecclesiastical establishments, seminaries, and so on, in the quarter. With the whole of the Left-Bank given over increasingly to property speculation, it seems unlikely, however, that the small shop-keeper, the small workshop, the *vins-charbons* and restaurants of the type *chez Mimile* will long survive, if they have not already gone under. Little of the area is likely to be covered by protection orders that tend to neglect buildings of the 1820s, 1830s and 1840s; and two new streets have already been cut through the rue Mouffetard, breaking up the unity of the narrow, climbing street. In most of the adjoining streets, the original population is giving way to middle-class intellectuals and professional people; and the quiet provincialism of the rue Lhomond and the rue des Boulangers is rapidly being breached by a proliferation of expensive bars and *boutiques*, the Place de la Contrescarpe now having become as much a tourist attraction as the sad little Place du Tertre in Montmartre. The whole area is even more threatened by the proliferation of Universities and the consequent politisation of a quarter that, from being a centre of conspiracy in the 1820s and 1830s, entered into a dormant clericalism during the Third Republic. Neither Simenon nor Maigret would find their way about the quartier Mouffetard now; it has changed almost beyond recognition, and very much for the worse.

21 5 rue Geoffroy Saint-Hilaire, Vme.
The building housing the eighteenth-century official responsible to the Lieutenant-Criminel for the policing of the old horse market, Faubourg Saint-Marceau, built in the reign of Louis XV and classified as a historical monument. This is the only eighteenth-century building included. It seemed a suitable introduction to one of the particularities of the *Vme arrondissement* throughout the nineteenth century, as a quarter closely associated with the horse trade, inherited from the previous century, the horses coming in from the west, from the Perche, their sale confined to this unruly southern quarter.

22 Hire of horses, 9 rue Geoffroy Saint-Hilaire, Vme.
Another reminder of the nineteenth-century vocation of this part of the old Faubourg Saint-Marceau, in fading lettering.

23 Menuiserie, 29 rue Poliveau, Vme.
A small workshop in the Vme, off the rue
Geoffroy Saint-Hilaire, in a deep yard
adjoining a tiny house, the ground-floor
humming with machinery, the single
upper room apparently a bedroom, the
house itself of rural proportions.

24 Doorway, 35 rue Poliveau, Vme.
The doorway, First Empire or
Restoration, with the monogram of the
owner in ironwork in the centre, the
entry long since condemned, though the
small house is still inhabited, being
approached from a more modest entry
to the right. The condemned door
bottle green.

25   A courtyard leading off the rue Poliveau, Vme.
The walls dripping with damp, the steep stairs leading
up to the single storey on the right, the small house
hidden from the street by an apartment house in
yellow brick, H. B. M., built in the late 1920s.

26 Café Bar, 30 rue Poliveau, Vme.

An October afternoon in the rue Poliveau, a quiet street of small workshops, one- and two-storeyed houses, in an area of the Vme as yet untouched by the tourist trade and by wealthy intellectuals. The two *retraités* with time on their hands — it is 3 p.m. — appear to be *habitués*; they belong to a fast-disappearing generation of *porteurs de bérets*. With luck, this part of the Vme may see them out, as it is at a safe distance from Censier and from Maubert-Mouffetard and the Montagne Sainte-Geneviève.

27 Rue Geoffroy Saint-Hilaire, Vme.

Second Empire fountain near the entrance to the Jardin des Plantes, with dolphins, ivy-covered, and falling leaves.

28 Yawning lion, entry to the Jardin des Plantes, Vme.

A very lazy, very bored lion, pretending to be in the jungle of the Ile-de-France, guarding the entrance to the Jardin des Plantes, the preserve of elderly card-players and of children off from school.

29 Le cèdre de Jussieu, Jardin des Plantes, Vme
The finest tree in Paris, safe from the wholesale
destruction of trees on the boulevards and public
squares, cut down to make way for the traffic and
underground *parkings*. The plant was brought from
London in Jussieu's three-cornered hat. The tree is on
a hillock—a *butte*—formed by an eighteenth-century
rubbish dump, an easy climb for week-end couples,
enabling the girl to lean heavily on the arm of her
cavalier during the upward climb.

30 Card players, Jardin des Plantes, Vme.

More of the *béret*ed generation, enjoying the afternoon October sun, under the glass roof of the botanic building, the principal Parisian haven of the elderly *économiquement faibles,* from the less fashionable areas of the Vme, and, more numerous, from the neighbouring XIIIme.

31 Jardin des Plantes, Vme.
A younger enthusiast among the card-players.

32   Card players, Jardin des Plantes, Vme.
And a reminder that the Paris *Mosque* is just the other side of the road, in the deep rue Geoffroy Saint-Hilaire, the man on the left and his three French companions unconcerned by racial problems or by memories of a recent war.

33   Jardin des Plantes, Vme
With the Buttes-Chaumont, the Jardin des Plantes is the most democratic of Paris open spaces. A further study of concentration of a younger enthusiast.

34 Jardin des Plantes, Vme.
Intense concentration on clubs, the lady playing the nine, the old man without a hat holding in reserve the alarming queen. The park chairs are mobilised as tables, contributing to the closeness of concentration.

35 Jardin des Plantes, Vme.
Late afternoon in October, a cross-section of
generations, with students from Censier and the
Halle-aux-Vins, *lycéens* and *lycéennes* on their way
home, a little African boy, and a father baby-sitting.

RIGHT
37 Jardin des Plantes, Vme.
Yet another activity of the Jardin. A Thursday
afternoon, the *monitrice* in action with whistle and
briskly shouted orders, dressed in a blue and white
track-suit, the French more than ever *fervents de la
culture physique*, a relic of the *Front Populaire* and of
Vichy.

36 Jardin des Plantes, Vme.
The *pères tranquilles* and the *mères tranquilles*
concentrate on the cards laid out on the folding park
chairs; the younger generation concentrate still lower
down, at ground level, on marbles.

38   **Children in the Jardin des Plantes, Vme.**

**39   Courtyard with washing, 30 rue des
Boulangers, Vme.**
The lady at her front door, having just put out her
Tuesday's washing and having changed, for our
benefit, into the flowered *tablier*. Her street is still safe
from American tourists and from the French
intellectuals who have invaded the quartier
Mouffetard, the rue des Boulangers still justifying its
name as a street of nineteenth-century artisans.

40 Courtyard off the rue Mouffetard, Vme.
The rue Mouffetard itself has been transformed in the
course of the last ten years, the small shops and cafés
replaced by *boutiques*, antique-shops, *discos* and
pizzerias, the artisans and the Algerians driven out to
make way for readers of *Charlie-Hebdo*. There are
great gaps in the street; but a few courtyards still offer
the appearance of tranquillity.

41 Off the rue Mouffetard, Vme.
A Louis-Philippe entry off a courtyard, catching the
six o'clock October sun.

42 Off the rue Mouffetard, Vme.
A communal tap, in the same courtyard, a witness to
1848, perhaps even to the *Quatre Sergents de la
Rochelle*, commemorated by an inn–sign a little further
up the street.

43 Coutellerie, 102 rue Mouffetard, Vme.
A proud survivor of the old rue Mouffetard and its
Sunday morning street market, before the tourists and
the *gauchistes* moved in. The shop is on the steep
slope leading to the once-provincial, secluded place de
la Contrescarpe. It is a family firm, of Auvergnat
origin, and with the full range—*toute la batterie* in
fact—of local industry from Laguiole, in the Aveyron,
the old capital of knives. On the left, a narrow *entrée*
to a nineteenth-century alley, connecting with the rue
Lhomond.

44 Bois Charbons, 6 rue de l'Arbalète, Vme.
Survivors of the old quartier Mouffetard, the one carrying a shopping-bag, in front of a *bougnat,* one of the remaining strongholds of a once-artisanal Vme. They have just left the café, after a 6 p.m. drink, and are concluding a conversation in the quiet street.

45 Cordonnerie, 12 rue de l'Arbalète, Vme.
Another survivor. After his retirement, there will not be a *reprise,* the *fonds de commerce* will be sold, the premises taken over by a bar or a *pizzeria.* It is nearly 7 p.m., and the *cordonnier* is still at work, while enjoying an evening chat.

46   Corner of the rue Lhomond 60, and the place Lucien Herr, Vme.
Just around the corner, the restaurant *Chez Mimile*,
the owner, long dead, from Decazeville, the restaurant
carried on by his widow and his daughter, Mimile
himself a *peintre du dimanche*; in the middle of the
balustrade, the entry to a quiet nineteenth-century
house with a courtyard shady with acacias, the one-
time home of some Parisian Tartarin.

3

XXme arrondissement:
Belleville-Ménilmontant.

. . . Elle entra, un peu plus loin, dans une petite papeterie-mercerie,
à la devanture de laquelle s'epoussiéraient des réglisses, des Pères La
Colique, des bobines de fil et des publications illustrées gauloises ou
enfantines. Des soldats de plomb éclopés se menaçaient de leurs sabres
ou de leurs fusils tordus tandis que jaunissaient à en roussir
d'authentiques images d'Epinal. A l'extérieur, des pinces à linge
proposaient aux passants les journaux du jour. La marchande se tenait
habituellement dans son arrière-boutique et accourait au son du
carillon . . .

RAYMOND QUENEAU, *Pierrot mon ami*, 1943

. . . Il alla prendre l'apéritif à un petit café dont la tranquille terrasse
s'articulait à l'angle de deux rues. Puis il déjeuna dans un restaurant,
petit aussi, presque aussi petit que le café . . .

RAYMOND QUENEAU, *Pierrot mon ami*, 1943

. . . Elle [rue de Belleville] va du Faubourg du Temple à la porte des
Lilas. Les rues des deux arrondissements [XIXme and XXme] y
viennent jeter leurs eaux boueuses, leurs eaux de pauvreté. Numéros
pairs, le vingtième; impairs, le dix-neuvième. Divisions administratives
qui tiennent aussi peu de place dans la réalité que dans mon esprit. Il y
a ici une Internationale de la misère. Belleville et Ménilmontant . . .

EUGÈNE DABIT, *Faubourgs de Paris*, 1933

THE XXme is an area that lends itself to superlatives, because it *is* dramatic. It is the most Parisian of any *arrondissement*, in the sense, first of all, that it is still the fortress-stronghold of *le titi parisien*, the skilled artisan, the female *arpète*, and of pretty well the whole cross-section of the *petit peuple*. Along with the industrial suburbs that spread northwards below its north-facing slopes, onto the Pays de France and the Parisis, it is the true home of Paris speech, of the long 'a's and of a confident vulgarity that excels in disrespect. It is the highest part of the city and probably still one of the healthiest, at least towards the Télégraphe and the Pyrénées. It certainly has a much stronger, more binding, more lasting collective identity than even the old quartier de la Bastille (*la Bastoche*); and this it has inherited from the repeated violence of a nineteenth-century revolutionary past, and that has managed to survive in a period of successive waves of immigration, bringing to its heights Russian and Polish Jews, Algerians, Senegalese, indeed the territory of *La vie devant soi*, of Madame Rosa, Ajar's delightful populist novel (and Belleville has been the subject of many previous populist novels). Geographically it is distinctive, an area cascading in many steps and steep rural streets, tiny courtyards, individual houses with leafy gardens, and semi-visible shacks and cottages nestling against the high railing of the *ceinture*. Its history is in its proud memory of independence and past defiance, in its many early-nineteenth-century buildings, rather than in *monuments historiques*—the only one that comes to mind is the *fontaine Henri IV*. It is the terrain par excellence of the skilled artisan and the small workshop, but it also houses a few smallish factories. There used to be both barracks and their concomitant, brothels; both have gone, leaving only the indication of street names and the washable fronts of former *maisons closes*. The rue des Amandiers—what is left of it—is a crumbling museum of the Paris of 1848, of the *hardis compagnons*, as well as of the Commune. But traditional Belleville has not long to go; the property speculators, the high-rise blocks are closing in from two directions, from down below and from the top, so that its skyline is already altered, and the blocks are soon occupied by middle-class professional people, young couples from the provinces. Some areas, Métro Belleville, are still unaffected; but, rue Orfila, the bulldozers and the cranes are already at work.

47 115 rue des Amandiers, XXme.
Rather a depressing start, at the bottom end of the XXme, Belleville-Ménilmontant, rue des Amandiers, with its tiny two-storeyed houses visibly threatened with demolition. The tiny *café-hôtel* on the right has red and white check curtains, to match the napkins: *Au Bon Accueil*. It looks as if, next door, *Lisette* is about to sell out; but one hopes it may be just the autumn sales. The street, till recently the most striking survival of mid-nineteenth-century working-class Belleville-Ménilmontant, in the morning sun, is already displaying an alarming number of gaps.

48 111 rue des Amandiers, XXme.
Serrurier A. Bureau au fond de la Cour. The dustbin men have been; but the *Etablissements Bordelais* are in no hurry to open, while the *loge* of the *concierge* on the left sleeps behind closed steel shutters. There is no sign of life on the first floor either. It is about 7.45. The *Deux Pièces* advertised is in the neighbourhood, Métro Couronnes.

49 Cycles Sport, corner of the rue Sorbier, XXme.

Halfway up the steep XXme, with its many steps and little rural climbing streets, a cycle shop, to attract *les gars de Belleville,* the young mechanics and apprentices, tempting them with *vélomoteurs* or powerful, thunderous motorcycles, on which to attack the heights, rue du Télégraphe, or, at weekends, to thunder down, *à la conquête de Paris,* in tight groups, to the République and the portes Saint-Martin and Saint-Denis, the old pleasure spots, the very centre of the city for the Bellevillois and the Bellevilloises, Parisian traditionalists, for whom the point of entry is still the triumphal arches of forgotten armies and forgotten victories.

50 Entry to rue Juillet, XXme.
A rural street, hinting of summer, on the middle slopes of Belleville, shuttered houses, dating back to Louis-Philippe, before Belleville was incoporated in Paris, the homes of independent artisans, market-gardeners, shop-keepers and small tradesmen.

RIGHT

51 Rue de la Voulzie, XXme.
A narrow cutting, with old *pavé,* draining off the water down the middle, between an abandoned electric lightbulb factory on the left, and a tall house rumbling with machinery on the right, a relic of semi-industrial Belleville, *Budapest* crying out about something or other, overtopped by shrubbery, in an abandoned garden.

52 Upper detail of 7 rue Westermann, XXme.
Union Populaire, and the lower part of the old ochre-coloured house rumbling with machinery, the upper storeys, with green raffia blinds, inhabited, with clothing hanging from a window, the street commemorating a guillotined revolutionary general from Alsace, certainly a stranger to the heights.

53 Doorway to staircase, courtyard of 7 rue Westermann, XXme.
In the courtyard of the same house, the inviting doorway, with its mat, the *minuterie* to the right, leading up, a well-worn step, old wooden staircase curling round, up the four storeys of a tall house, in a quarter where the early-nineteenth-century buildings reach high. The threshold to a private history, written, rarely, in the staccato reports of the *chronique judiciare,* but more often unrecorded and only to be guessed at.

54   Courtyard in sunshine, early morning, 26 rue Villiers-de-l'Isle-Adam, XXme.
The bright October sun, brightening an east-facing wall, early in the morning, 7.30 or 8, of a two-storeyed house, the shutters closed, the green raffia blinds down, the inhabitants still in bed, two pots of geraniums witnessing to a groping domesticity and care, among handsome early-nineteenth-century railings, a provision of spare chimney pots, a beer bottle abandoned in the forecourt, greasy paper blowing in the gusts of wind in this high place, a bare façade of old uneven bricks, private lives hidden from the street.

55   Restaurant A La Bonne Humeur, 26 rue Orfila, XXme.

A La Bonne Humeur, and it is indeed, midday or a little later, paper tablecloths, an open bottle of *vin ordinaire* to each table, the tables crowded mostly with housepainters and building workers in white smocks, Fernand at the bar, his black hair brushed down and coming to a point in the middle of a low forehead, making him look like a 1900 boxer or oarsman, his face lined with smiles, his 'a's very long, Raymonde, a large woman with very blonde hair, bringing the food, conversation *à la cantonnade*, jokes flying across the room like billiard-balls, pigeon holes for thirty or forty napkin rings, *restaurant d'habitués*, open for lunch only.

57   Rue Orfila, XXme.

Country shutters, peeling, as to be
seen in the villages of the Ile-de-
France, a reminder of the rusticity of
Belleville, once noted for its
salubrious air, and, in the early-
nineteenth century, still a summer
retreat for well-to-do Parisians from
down below.

BELOW

**58   General view of the rue Laurence Savart,
XXme.**

A semi-rural street, running steeply down towards the
bottom end of Ménilmontant, lined with small square
houses, some behind small gardens, like *maisons de
retraités* in a provincial town, the peace of the street
already threatened by the construction of high-rise
apartment blocks at the bottom end, and uneven
pavé still eluding the planner.

LEFT

**56   Glimpse through doorway, 32
rue Orfila, XXme.**

Vue plongeante, through several levels,
the narrow entry, a dark staircase,
the brass knob of the elaborate *rampe*
catching the sun from the street, then
down four steps, to the entrance to the
workshop of Michel Nomary, *artisan*,
an independent Bellevillois, of a type
still surviving, from the time of the
Paris Commune, the violence,
heroism, enthusiasm and suddenness
of which had all at once emerged
from such semi-secret, independent
places, and later the homes of
bricoleurs, of inventors, of artisans
who built motorcars or who put
aeroplanes together, in the early
years of the century, and who could
turn their skills to almost anything,
including the manufacture of
weapons.

59 Entry to house, 12 rue Laurence Savart, XXme.

The entrance to a small house in the same street, an elaborate letter-box, the promise of a small garden and an upper window with the shutter open, the quiet home of a contented life, each detail denoting care and placidity and an embattled privacy. One is surprised at the absence, on the iron gate, of *Chien méchant*.

60 3 rue Laurence Savart, XXme.

Another house in the same small-town street, further down, nearer the threatening border of the invading apartment blocks, but still serene in petit-bourgeois or artisanal contented independence, a house of cats and canaries, of potted plants, hiding behind its railings, keeping itself to itself, one would like to think the safe refuge of *le père tranquille*, of *Hulot*, doing his shopping in slippers.

61 Courtyard leading off opposite 11 rue Boyer, XXme.
The house on the left is approached by five steps between elaborate railings, the entry, just visible, behind the invading jungle of ivy, surmounted by a porch of the type to be seen in the small market towns of the Ile-de-France; there is a blanket hanging from an upper window.

62   25 rue Boyer, La Bellevilloise, XXme.

. . . Quelques pas encore et voici la Bellevilloise, coopérative communiste . . .
Eugène Dabit, *Faubourgs de Paris,* 1933

Just opposite the country courtyard, the entrance to a more recent, more public, less individualistic, more organised Belleville, the ironwork of the doors unmistakably 1927, the plinth a reminder of the still persistent strength of the P.C.F., on the heights, especially among the immigrant population. The bourgeois poodle has likewise just committed itself politically, in a puddle on the very threshold of *la Bellevilloise.*

63 6 rue des Cascades, XXme.
The diamond-pierced shutters, like eyes enabling the
suspicious rustic to look outwards, by standing on a
chair, seem depressingly closed, the peeling walls, in
an advanced stage of leprosy indicate a decay beyond
repair, the black entry is hopeless and uninviting; but
the plants in the window sills of the upper storey
suggest that there is life yet and that demolition may
be delayed. Elections are—as always—imminent.

64 Remouleur (spelt wrong) with bell, probably rue des Cascades, XXme.

There are not many left; and, either because he is much in demand, because of his rarity, or because he travels far in search of custom, he is very mobile. The next day we met him far away in the Xme, with his bell, his poor spelling, and his rubber-tyred workshop. He looks like an Auvergnat; he is certainly not a Parisian. The XXme is a favourable terrain for independent artisans of his kind.

65 The knife-grinder again, with full equipment in action, rue des Cascades, XXme.

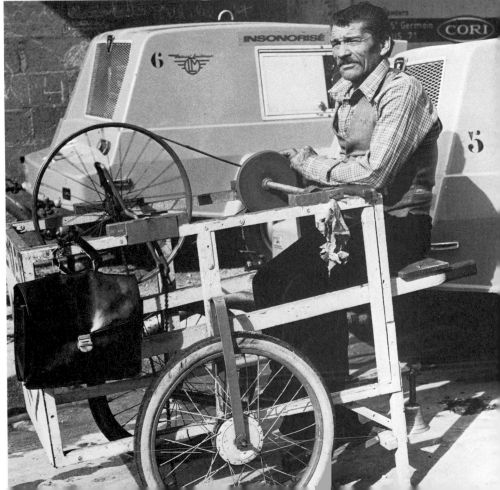

66 Off the rue de la Mare opposite the rue de Savies, XXme.

A glimpse of two old houses, early-nineteenth-century, partly hidden by shrubbery and a sinister temporary wall that seems to spell out impending demolition, yet still showing many signs of life: the green raffia blinds rolled up, in a couple of windows, open to the October sun, most of the shutters back (though two are closed, perhaps a sign of impending departure), a pigeon perched on the edge of an open dormer window (*mansarde*), a window-box at the one next to it, yet another reminder of the Parisian concern for flowers and plants, already discernible in the reports of eighteenth-century *juges de paix* and *commissaires* on the subject of dangerously placed flower-pots and window-boxes. The first-floor room of the house on the right has a fine balcony. But the view is spoilt by the hideous threat rising above the two old houses and their red-tiled roofs.

RIGHT

67 Rue de Savies, looking down towards the rue de la Mare, XXme.

The still rural slopes of Belleville-Ménilmontant, reaching down to the level of the *petite ceinture*, in its cutting, increasingly the frontier between a still individualistic, artisanal, provincial north-east Paris, and the new apartment blocks of an approaching professional middle-class, as, a century after the Commune, it approaches gingerly the heights from below. The small café (plate 69) is at the bottom right, the two tiny houses (plate 68) on the left.

68   55 and 56 rue de la Mare, XXme.
Adjoining houses, both occupied. An Algerian with a
scarlet rug knocked on the door of the nearer one, was
let in, spending a quarter of an hour inside, then
emerging still with the rug. The house on the right
has a shop on the ground-floor no longer in use, but
furnished as a sitting-room.

69   Au Bon Coin, on the corner of rue Pixérécourt and rue de la Mare.

Why Pixérécourt, the Directory playwright of the Boulevards, should be commemorated up here I do not know. There is a single customer inside, seated at a wooden table, writing in purple ink. The *patron*, in a blue apron, is washing glasses behind the bar. Behind him a corkscrew staircase leads up to his bedroom, one shutter of which is open. It is four in the afternoon, and there is a general somnolence. The two pots of plants, like formal statues of saints or heralds, lend a sort of *facteur Cheval* dignity to this small temple of individualism, provincialism and tranquillity. The patron, like *le Caïd* in MacOrlan's *Tradition de Minuit*, lives and sleeps above his work. Maigret would at once feel at ease here. But the quiet is already threatened by the encroaching apartment blocks glimpsed to the left of one of the pots. How long will such two-storeyed havens of regular habit remain undisturbed in a cycle dating from the 1920s?

70   Blanchisserie, 31 rue de l'Ermitage, XXme.

Another small shop gone. Whatever happens, there will be no more washing taken in here, and the small *blanchisseries*, returning the shirts pinned up in pink paper, the collars given cardboard supports, are making way for the *laveries mécaniques*. The paling letters in dark red, still just visible, seem to spell out the steady erosion of artisanal Paris.

71   Marchand de Couleurs, 92 rue de Ménilmontant, XXme.

But here, on the busy rue de Ménilmontant, as it rises steeply, on the route of the *96* (*la ligne des Montagnes*), the central street of the village, *le petit commerce* still flourishes, in a quarter that once gave as much support to Pierre Poujade as to the P.C.F. The *marchand de couleurs* is not merely a colourful emporium, with its pots of paint and its bright yellow dusters, it also smells agreeably of shoe polish, floor polish, wax, lamp oil. There is provision for the window box and the small garden; there is even a small round *château-fort* in yellow bricks that awaits its gnome or its china rabbit. Cups and plates can be repaired as well as umbrellas. Busts of historical figures and cherubs and Swiss barometers are on display. There are three large cats on the counter, in the dark, cool, aromatic interior.

RIGHT

73   Bridge over the line of the ceinture, end of rue de la Mare, XXme.

The rue de la Mare has started to run out, forced into a narrow *impasse* as it encounters the elaborate, *art-nouveau* railings protecting the railway-line of *la petite ceinture*, crossed by an even more elaborate bridge, now closed to the public. The *ceinture* marks the XXme, as the *métro aérien* marks other *arrondissements*, providing its inhabitants with reassuring night rumblings, as goods trains and sleeping-cars pass on their mysterious 4 a.m. journeys, bearing the sleeper on the Italian express from the Gare de Lyon to the Gare du Nord, all unknown to him, through the deep cutting of Ménilmontant.

72   Stairway onto the street, 27 rue de la Mare, XXme.

A Louis-Philippe series of steps up from the street, protected by a solid, sensible, yet elegant iron balustrade, well-worn from the confident or hesitant steps of a hundred and forty years, and that seems to add dignity, even an air of drama, to the simple act of going up or coming down, as though each step in either direction were important, were part of the unstated rules of popular étiquette: *franchir le seuil*, of commitment on which there could be no going back. The steps are inviting: come up, they say, without giving any hint of what the darkness beyond may offer. Steps that perhaps have lost their true function: to display to full advantage an elegant pair of legs in long boots or tight trousers or to give attention to the small, hesitant foot, as it feels its way down. The cool balustrade is agreeable to the touch.

74   Entry to house, 7 impasse de la Mare, XXme.
The semi-concealed entrance, the flounced curtains of
its door denoting care, just approachable, through
thick shrubbery, of a peeling grey house, from the
impasse, crammed between two sets of railings. As the
house has a number, presumably the *facteur* comes this
way, if the owner of the two clothes lines ever receives
any mail. By day, the *impasse* is like a deep country
lane, lost in Paris; but at night it might be alarming.

**75   La maison du sauvage, 9 impasse de la
Mare, XXme.**
Next-door to the flounced curtain is *la maison du
sauvage*, a Parisian hermit and *original*, who, far from
seeking visitors to his retreat between the *impasse* and
the railway line, has taken care to barricade his home:
there are seven locks on the door and a series of
messages, none of them welcoming. Just to make sure,
there is a large board carrying DEFENSE
D'ENTRER in black painted letters, just discernible
between the leaves. But the *sauvage* is also artistic;
there are scallop shells arranged in patterns in wooden
boxes and china eggs in circles decorate the top of an
oil-drum. It is a very private, very cared-for domain,
with a mat in front of the much-padlocked door, its
windows covered inside with old checked material
that looks like a bedspread, to conceal the interior
from prying eyes. The *sauvage* intends to keep himself
to himself. He is at the end of the *impasse*, there is
nothing beyond. His privacy is guarded with the
elaborate defensive mechanism of a medieval *château-
fort*. Perhaps he is a *châtelain*.

76 Upper view of houses overlooking the ceinture, from the impasse de la Mare, XXme.
The upper storey of a tiny house, perhaps that of the *sauvage*, more likely one next-door, a chimney-pot indicating that the owner has a coke stove, the closed shutters giving no more away than the curtained front-door in the previous picture. Rising high above the home of the *sauvage* or of his neighbour, two steep houses, in the afternoon sunlight, well above the intense vegetation of the *sauvage*'s Parisian jungle, rising to six or seven storeys, the windows protected with rumpled green raffia blinds, as in a print of 1848 or the Commune—these windows have no doubt witnessed both— the small windows lighting a staircase in the house on the right. The houses face over the gulf in which runs the *ceinture*, onto modern blocks of flats that know nothing of nineteenth-century history.

77 Courtyard, impasse de la Mare, from the other side, XXme.
The tall houses facing onto the *ceinture* contain a country courtyard full of pots and espaliers, with an old green seat that looks as if it had been borrowed from a country station, behind the screen of ivy and climbing plants.

78 Courtyard, impasse de la Mare, XXme.
The courtyard from the other side, an electric washer
in a rural setting, a china swan gazing out from
behind the grilled window, the lady very neat and
houseproud, talkative and not at all *sauvage*. The last
we see of the impasse de la Mare.

80 View of the ceinture, from the bridge, level of 68 rue de Ménilmontant, XXme.
The gulley through which runs the mystery railway of Paris, the *ceinture,* as seen from the bridge of the rue de Ménilmontant, the closed *art-nouveau* bridge at the end of the rue de la Mare in the mid-distance, the foliage of the *impasse* to the right, completing hiding from this central observatory, on which people constantly come and go, the *maison du sauvage* and those of his neighbours. The platform of an abandoned station, one no longer marked on any map of Paris, where no train will stop, no-one will alight, and past which, in the worst night hours—4, 4.30— may rumble ghastlily whistling goods trains, or, pulled slowly by shunting engines, the blue and gold sleeping cars of the *Compagnie Internationale des Wagons Lits des Grands Express Européens,* as the sleepers stir uneasily in this Parisian limbo, a secret *réseau* connecting the main stations, or following itineraries known only to those concerned with unobtrusive nocturnal transport. As if to emphasise the fact, the line at this point emerges from a tunnel that runs under much of the hilly XXme.

LEFT

79 Courtyard, 28 rue Henri Chevreau, XXme.
Perhaps more than anything so far, the very expression of Belleville-Ménilmontant, cascading downwards, in a series of irregular steps and tiny platforms, an up-and-down geography less dramatic, but more intimate, than the *Montées* of semi-southern Lyon. At the open entrance to the staircase of the house at the top, a Tunisian and his two small children.

81 104 rue des Amandiers, XXme.
The rue des Amandiers, fast disappearing, once the centre of the Belleville artisan, now, in what remains, mostly inhabited by Algerians. A clothes' shop, dresses in bright colours and garish patterns, to attract the Algerian and Tunisian girls.

82 Rue Soleillet, XXme.
La Lampe Rationnel (sic) *Fabrique de Lampes*, one of the rare factories in Belleville, a quarter primarily of small workshops and independent skilled artisans: this is no doubt one of the sources of the strength of the P.C.F. in this area of north-east Paris.

83 6 rue des Partants, XXme.
A sad little café, with little time to go, long since deprived of a military clientèle, the last *partants* certainly dating back to 1914 or so, a hang-over from the nineteenth century, when Belleville had been still thought of as potentially dangerous.

84 19 rue des Partants, XXme.
Au Bon Goût will not reopen, the rue des Partants already has the mark of death about it.

85 13 rue des Partants, XXme.
Judging from the washable tiles, a sure indication of brothel architecture, a *maison close* as late as the 1930s, a throw-back to the military vocation of the now decaying street.

RIGHT
86 Passage des Mûriers, XXme.
The *passage* as it runs downwards, between the dwellings of mid-nineteenth-century artisans, now mostly the crowded homes of immigrants.

LEFT

87 Passage des Mûriers, XXme.
A study in colour, a peeling, suppurating ochre wall,
lépreux indeed, sick and sweating with damp, the
background to a blood-red Algerian rug as it hangs
out of an open window, Barbey-d'Aurevilly's *rideau
cramoisi* in a Belleville setting, hanging out like a flag
of revolt, in fact just airing in what meagre sun can
penetrate the passage des Mûriers, the latter a very
distant memory, for there are no bushes anywhere in
sight, the colour of the rug reflected in the darker
scarlet, like very old, dried thick blood, of the appeal
to demonstrate, *Métro Charonne;* but the walls take
up a more private, schoolboy quarrel or joke, on the
subject of Red-Head who also squints, as does his
mother, started high up, just below the lamp,
abandoned unfinished, and started again and
completed at a more manageable level.

88 Boy in window, 2 rue des Pruniers, XXme

89 Coiffure, 14 rue des Mûriers, XXme.
A petrified Michèle Morgan, her head enveloped in a
headscarf, *en matière gazeuse,* and tied loosely under
the chin, as for the promenade deck of an Ocean-
going liner, looks out blindly at the declining rue des
Mûriers, with less interest or curiosity than the small
Algerian child in the previous picture. A potted plant
keeps her company. The pleated curtains are
touchingly provincial, as are the two shop-fronts, the
street itself, still offered some hope, at least as
indicated by the building activity of the rope and the
bucket.

90   Au Petit Boucher, 45 rue des Amandiers, XXme.

Like many another *Au Petit Boucher,* personal service, the exchange of information withing a narrow periphery, and, to outdo *Coiffure, two* potted plants.

RIGHT

91   2 rue Duris, XXme.

Another, more modest *marchand de couleurs,* giving a closer view, this time, of a prancing horse, a china Mickey Mouse, and a cluster of large rubber balls dimly seen hanging from the ceiling, shopping-bags, the inimitable black *cabas.*

92 Algerian girl, corner of rues Duris and des Amandiers, XXme.
She insisted on getting in, at the entrance to *Alimentation Générale*, a corner shop, trying not to laugh, and wearing *Petit Bateau* trousers.

93 Alimentation Générale, 1 rue Duris.
The corner shop, rue Duris and rue des Amandiers, with an elaborate Louis-Philippe ironwork above the door. The Algerian girl went with the shop, we had to take her first.

94   Fabrique de Banjos, 9 rue Duris, XXme.
There is a lot going on, not just as indicated by the peeling letters of
the *Serrurerie-Ferronnerie*: shopfronts, steel grills, balconies, stair-
rails, blinds, something else that has almost disappeared, but also,
down the dark passageway leading off No 9, *Fabrique de Banjos, V.
Jacobacci, Au Fond de la Cour. Au Fond de la Cour* is the litany of the
artisanal XXme, as well as of some other *arrondissements*. It denotes a
dimension of Paris that is not immmediately apparent, that has to be
sought out, and that is nearly always worth seeking out.

95   Courtyard, 7–9 rue Duris
The banjos are presumably at the bottom. Corsets and
brassières are half-way down on the right, an
imposing figure with a long scarf is on the left.

96   Courtyard, 7–9 rue Duris XXme.
The window beside *F bis* is protected by flowered
curtains. There is a basin with washing covered over
with a plastic cloth near the entry to *F bis*.

97   Courtyard, 7–9 rue Duris XXme.
What appears to be a one-roomed house, approached by a narrow door made out of a shutter, in the same courtyard. The plants outside are for the enjoyment of all, expressing trust and neighbourliness.

98   23 rue Duris, XXme.
Another brothel converted to a different purpose. The washable tiles are in elaborate mosaics, hinting of the late 1930s and *l'année de l'Expo* (1937). The oldest profession has given way to *couscous*, a commentary on the 60s and 70s, on Algerian post-independence. In this quarter, the restaurant, which is also a take-away one (*à emporter*) may well cater to a predominantly Algerian and Tunisian clientèle. The prices, however, are not up-to-date.

99 Corner of 33 rue Duris and the rue des Amandiers, XXme.
In the foreground, an 1840s shopfront. The *Hôtel du Cantal*, in fading letters, is a
reminder of the massive influx of the casual labour force, including building,
carrying, and casual work, of young men from the Cantal and the Aveyron
throughout the first half of the nineteenth century, many of them housing
together in cheap hotels and *meublés* in Belleville, while working in the developing
quarters of western Paris, returning to the heights in the evenings, their place
taken, in the present century, by Algerians, Tunisians and Portuguese. But the
Hôtel du Cantal is probably doomed, there are already great gaps in the street.

100   Hôtel du Rendez-vous, 28 rue des Cendriers, XXme.
It looks as if it might be living up to its name, with the open door and the dark staircase to the right. The café has an elegant Louis-Philippe shop front.

101   47 rue des Cendriers, XXme.
An Algerian boy in front of a sad little shop, the potted plants disguising whatever function it may serve. In the windows reflected by the evening light are the outlines of the new modern flats that are steadily replacing nineteenth-century Ménilmontant.

RIGHT
102   Courtyard off the rue des Cendriers, XXme.
Impenetrable graffiti, a carriage stone, the door-shutter latched back, and a little *imprimerie* at the far end, a habitual denizen of courtyards ever since the days of Marat in the still existing *Cour du Commerce*. The present one will specialise in visiting cards, *faire-parts*, handsheets and advertisements.

103 Rue des Cendriers, XXme.

An elegant shop-front, in dark bottle green, neat billowing muslin curtains, the handle removed from the door, and unlikely ever to be inserted there again, the blind fixed back in the immobility of death: so that one is unlikely to hear again the happy, creaking sound of the *store* as it is gradually lowered for a new day, the promise of continuity. A suitable note no doubt on which to conclude a circular walk through disappearing nineteenth-century Belleville-Ménilmontant.

4

Xme arrondissement:
quartier du canal Saint-Martin and quartier du Faubourg Saint-Martin.

. . . Depuis deux ans, Pierrot habitait le même hôtel, *l'hôtel de l'Aveyron,* une bâtisse d'un matériau léger et à un seul étage, avec un balcon extérieur qui faisait communiquer entre elles les différentes chambres. La cour était une ancienne cour de ferme, une lucarne donnait vue sur un jardin de couvent . . .

RAYMOND QUENEAU, *Pierrot mon ami,* 1943

. . . A sept heures, on ferme. Valentin enlève la clenche et décarre. Il ne met les volets que vers neuf heures, après le dîner. A sept heures cinq, il entre au café des Amis, rue de Wattignies . . . On cause, il écoute. Il cause un peu aussi, pour ne pas avoir l'air distant. On parle de l'Expo 37 qui ne va peut-être pas ouvrir à cause des grèves, mais qui fera marcher le commerce si elle ouvre . . . On parle surtout de cyclisme, de foutballe et du perfectionnement de la race chevaline . . .

RAYMOND QUENEAU, *Le dimanche de la vie,* 1951

THE Xme is vast, central—or at least traditionally so—dilapidated, increasingly unfashionable, very varied, and largely unspoilt. There is little to connect the grands boulevards, quartier Bonne-Nouvelle, République, porte Saint-Denis and porte Saint-Martin with the watery world of the canal, of Dabit's *Hôtel du Nord*, the swing bridge, and the Grange-aux-Belles beyond. The canal imposes its own laws, dictating the location of many small industries, workshops and depots, giving to the quarter a regularly transient population of northerners and Belgians, and at the same time dividing the quarter as by a frontier, so that la Grange-aux-Belles seems almost foreign territory when approached from the near-side of the swing-bridge. This, the *pont-tournant*, and the steep humped footbridges near it, provide an observatory to the life and movement of the quarters on both quays. As if to maintain the low-lying harmony of canal land, most of the buildings on each side tend to be squat; and the rural proportions of many of the houses are further accentuated as one moves away from the canal towards the Faubourg Saint-Martin, an area which is also a maze of long, deep courtyards. This is an area of work rather than of residence, though a great many people do actually sleep here. Socially, this part of the *arrondissement*—indeed most of the rest of it—is rather disinherited, a fact that has undoubtedly contributed to the preservation of its predominantly early-nineteenth-century character, at one time terribly threatened by a project, favoured by M. Pompidou, to fill in the canal and convert it into a motorway (as has happened to the former canal de la Marne, at the porte de Charenton). So the canal is the lifeline of the quarter as it is, in more than one sense. Furthermore, there are no pleasure-spots, no buildings of historical interest, so that most of the *arrondissement* has succeeded in staying off the standard tourist routes; at best, the most the traveller is likely to see of it is the forecourt of the Gare du Nord, before he takes the *métro* or the bus. Though it contains three large hospitals, their presence has not brought into the area large numbers of doctors as residents. Socially it has thus remained an area inhabited above all by shop-keepers, artisans, *employés*, and immigrant workers. There does not seem much likelihood of it being overtaken by the sort of dandyfication that has devitalised the old IVme. The Xme is lucky enough not to have even a few yards of *voie piétonne*, its small streets remaining encumbered and untidy.

104 Café du Pont-Tournant, corner of the rue de la Grange-aux-Belles and the quai de Jemappes, seen from the bridge, Xme.
The *pont-tournant* (see plate 132) is the frontier between the two sides of the Xme, as divided by the canal Saint-Martin, the river link between Paris, the Nord, and the Belgian waterway system, linked by the canal de l'Ourcq. On one side, the conventional Xme, based on Strasbourg-Saint-Denis, on the further side, the rural sounding Grange-aux-Belles and Bichat. The two quays, quai de Valmy, quai de Jemappes, re-emphasise the link with the Nord and Belgium, as do the waterside cafés advertising *Stella-Artois* and *Ekla*, and the many barges carrying the Belgian tricolour. This is Simenon country, as well as the terrain of Eugène Dabit's *Hôtel du Nord*, a little further to the left, quai de Jemappes. The corner *Café du Pont-Tournant* is both an observatory and a frontier post, commanding the bridge; and the high building on the corner rises like a lighthouse or a signal station, at the entrance to the Grange-aux-Belles. It is early in the morning, 7.30–7.45, and soon there will be lines of small children, *cartables* on their back, as they head, holding parents hands, towards the *communale* on the near-side. As we spend half the day near the frontier, we will see them on the return journey, at midday, thus acquiring the sense of the movement of the quarter.

105   General view of lock, above the pont-tournant, Xme.
Facing northwards, towards the canal de l'Ourcq and
the water-link with Belgium, the steep footbridge in
the middle distance.

106   Ariane at the pont-tournant, Xme.

The *route du Nord* has always played the decisive role in the history and development of Paris and its surrounding Ile-de-France, linking both to the resources of the Nord and the Pas-de-Calais, the French coal basin and the products of the Belgian Provinces. The old water route predates the railway link by more than thirty years, with the opening of the Canal de l'Ourcq under the First Empire, helping to make Paris the leading port of France. The *mariniers*—the bargees—are either from the Nord or from Belgium, retaining from both the spotless pride in their floating homes, the neat check red and white table cloths and curtains, and the sense of comfort as a sort of compensation for the lowering greyness of Vlaminck's skies. This too is a threshold, as we look into the domesticity of *Ariane*'s bridge, the potted plants and the pipe-smoking patron, the muslin curtains and the stove-pipe of the kitchen, the checked curtained windows of the living quarters, and the television aerial enabling the floating family to follow the Tour de France and the *Stade Roubaisien*. *Ariane* is on its way from the main sand ports of Paris, quai de la Rapée and, on the left bank, quai de la Gare, which is also the port for the English coaster service *Paris-Londres*. The canal Saint-Martin is very much Maigret territory, one of the principal points of penetration, together with the Oise at Conflans-Sainte-Honorine, of Belgians and northerners.

LEFT
107 Ariane at the pont-tournant.
Ariane is about to pass through the lock, having taken on its load of sand, the footbridge in the middle distance.

108 87 quai de Valmy and end of rue Jean-Poulmarch, seen from bridge, Xme.
The other side of the footbridge, opposite la Grange-aux-Belles, looking towards the Louis-Philippard headquarters of the shoe-makers' union.

LEFT
109   Syndicat des Cordonniers, 21 rue Jean-Poulmarch, Xme.
A closer view of the *Fédération*, in a headquarters suggestive of an 1830 corner shop, surmounted by an elegant wooden lion and proud columns indicative of the survival of a *compagnonnage*, with its emphasis on artisanal skills and independence, rather than looking forwards to the powerful syndicalism of the C.G.T. There is something very early-nineteenth-century about the solid building, just as there is about the word *bottier*.

110   20 rue des Vinaigriers, Xme.
A near neighbour of the *Fédération de la Chaussure*, at the bottom of the steps leading from the quay and below water-level, a suitably Low Country topography, and another relic of a largely forgotten nineteenth-century enthusiasm. Who are the modern *Garibaldiens* and what do they do, in their headquarters that have, unfortunately, recently been given a modern shop-front? Do they wear red shirts and what rites do they perform, when they meet, behind discreet muslin curtains, rue des Vinaigriers?

111   Hôtel, 26 rue des Vinaigriers, Xme.
Surely one of the smallest hotels in Paris, even in the Xme, two rooms under a rural roof in red tiles, the ground-floor café now abandoned, though, judging from the open window, the first floor is still in business.

112   Restaurant de Bourgogne, 28 rue des Vinaigriers, Xme.

Jupiter, as well as Burgundy, to draw the Belgian custom from the canal nearby, for the rue des Vinaigriers is only just inland. Inside, there is much hilarity, engendered by the central table, laid, like the others, with a red cloth, and at which, nearer one than twelve, a wedding party has reached dessert and *digestifs* and is alternating between song: *Il ne faut pas rouler dessous la table*, and jokes in doubtful taste— *humour de commis-voyageur*—that send convulsions round the other tables, occupied, judging from the conversation from table to table, by regulars. The *plat du jour* is not Burgundian, but eminently Parisian; and suited to a *restaurant des chauffeurs: boeuf gros sel*, with leeks and *navets*. Most of the customers wear checked napkins, white and red, like the dotted curtains. There are twenty pigeon-holes for rings and napkins. A happy place in which we were received with smiles, amidst the side-splitting laughter of the wedding guests.

113 **Bar des Artisans, 23 rue des Vinaigriers, Xme.**

Magnificent Louis-Philippe lettering, to match the pride of the artisans, the elegance of the balconies, of the two doors and wide windows. The *Bar des Artisans* faces familiarly the *Restaurant de Bourgogne*. It is a friendly street.

LEFT

114   Bayoux, corner of rue des Recollets and quai de Valmy, Xme.
The sweeping curve of the quai de Valmy, the tall houses of the 1830s or 1840s below the level of the canal.

115   105 quai de Valmy, Xme.
A small hotel, its windows covered with green raffia blinds, and, beyond, the two-storeyed *Chez Henriette*, its menu examined with a view to an eventual visit.

LEFT

116 107 quai de Valmy, Xme.
A closer view of *Chez Henriette*, offering no indication
of Belgian clientèle, but advertising wrestling at the
old *Cirque d'Hiver*. It is early afternoon, lunch has
been served, and there is only one customer, his knees
visible from the street. The ground-floor window is
barred, perhaps a reminder that the quays of the canal
Saint-Martin are less reassuring at night than on a
sunny October afternoon, and that the canal itself
receives its regular quota of bodies, many of them,
two decades ago, those of Algerians of rival political
persuasions.

**117 Bonne-Chance on the canal, facing the
quai de Jemappes, Xme.**
Bonne-Chance, French or Belgian, on its way north,
out of Paris, with a full cargo, followed by another
barge that is empty. On the left, the workshops of the
low-lying quai de Jemappes.

118   Saint-Gérard negotiating the lock at the level of the pont-tournant, Xme.
The barge is high in the water and presumably empty, on its way to pick up a load at the port of Paris, quai de la Rapée and quai de la Gare (not a reference to Austerlitz, but in the pre-railway sense of *gare* meaning *port*).

119   Soudeur working on the lock gates, by the pont-tournant, Xme.
The windows of *Secours aux Noyés* can be seen in the background between the cluster of ivy and the hedge. The workman had come on work at the lock at 7.40.

120   Cadoricin, 49 rue Lucien-Sampaix, Xme.
Cadoricin and *Delsol*, to the accompaniment of accordion music, *bal-musette* style, on *Radio-Paris* advertising, in the 1930s, the fading reminder of a disappearing social history, on the cut-off end of a tall apartment house as if from a scene in a Carné film: *Shampooing Brillant à l'Huile*, and with something already indecipherable about hair. There used to a sung rhyme about *Cardoricin*, followed by the chorus *un meuble signé Lévitan est garanti pour longtemps*, transformed, during the War, by the French Section of the B.B.C. to: *Un Maréchal de 80 ans n'est pas garanti pour longtemps*. A reminder too that so much of the social history of Paris is fading away, in peeling blues and pinks, on the blind, cassata-like corners of desperately sad buildings. A small monument to the 20s and 30s.

LEFT

121 Lovers on bridge, quai de Valmy, Xme.
They were there at 2, and they were still there, having
scarcely moved, and having not spoken a word, in the
middle of their Chinese bridge, at 4.30, oblivious to
the movement of the canal, high up in the October
sun.

**122 102 quai de Jemappes, seen through the
lock at the level of the pont-tournant, rue de la
Grange-aux-Belles, Xme.**
The barge, on its way through the lock, with a load of
sand picked up quai de la Tournelle, the old river
gare, and still the principal port of Paris, is heading
north, towards the canal de l'Ourcq. Unlike most
barges in activity on the canal or on the Seine, it is
from Paris. Most are from the Somme, the Nord, the
Pas-de-Calais and Belgium .

123 Ambulances, 89 quai de Valmy, Xme.
Private ambulances, with a blue cross, and a feeble
up-and-down double note, not carrying much
conviction or sense of urgency, run from a former
shop on the ground-floor of an elegant 1830s house on
the quay, near the *pont-tournant*, in the afternoon sun.

124   Serrurerie, 10 rue de la Grange-aux-Belles, Xme.
Not *la clef des champs*, but the indication to the passer-by that, *au fond de la cour*, there is a locksmith. A handsome, old-fashioned key, of eighteenth-century shape and solidity.

125   Couleurs Bazar, 44 rue Bichat, XXme.
One of those long brooms used by street-cleaners to encourage the flow of water along the gutters or down the middle of the *pavé*. Queneau's Valentin could arm himself here with the instruments of his vocation as a sweeper.

126 Au Bon Vivant, 77 rue Bichat, Xme.
Mis-named, for, as a restaurant, long since dead,
though in fine lettering, on a peeling house, below the
level of the quayside, but still with signs of life on the
two upper floors. The lettering light pink on a
crumbling beige. The house is a survivor from early-
nineteenth-century rural Paris; but the house next-
door spells out the H.B.M. (*Habitations Bon Marché*)
efforts of the late 20s and early 30s, in a pattern of
bricks much in vogue from 1928 to the period of the
Front Populaire or even *l'Expo*. The steps lead up to
the level of the quai de Jemappes. There is a large
iron column for tying up a horse near the foot of the
steps.

**127 Etablissements Masson et Cie., 52 rue
Bichat, Xme.**
Opposite the defunct *Au Bon Vivant*, the approach to
a small workshop, metalwork, aluminium, with other
workshops on each side, approached by an 1840
plinthed entry. The lorry has broken down.
The photograph gives an eloquent sense of depth,
taking us right in, to the very bottom of the closed
arcade, *Les Ateliers R.C.*, so characteristic of the maze
of Louis-Philippe *passages* to be found at the other
end of the Xme, just north of the boulevard Bonne-
Nouvelle.

**128   Bridge over the canal, from the rue Bichat,
Xme.**
The lovers' Chinese bridge, approached from the
quayside, above the rue Bichat, facing onto the quai
de Valmy.

129 Rue Bichat, Xme.

130 Vieux papiers, rue Bichat, Xme.
Further afternoon activities, rue Bichat, with the light awaiting modernisation in the background, *vieux papiers, chiffons,* collected by an Algerian, in his lorry.

131 The pont-tournant, early in the morning, from the quai de Jemappes, Xme.
This is indeed the frontier post between the two halves of the Xme *arrondissement* as divided by the canal and the swing bridge, raised every half hour or so, as if to affirm the priority of in-coming and out-going water traffic, the *Café du Pont-Tournant* on the far side, early afternoon.

132 Seen through the window of the Café du Pont-Tournant, rue de la Grange-aux-Belles, Xme. The swing-bridge and the frontier post are just visible through the glassy leafage of an early-nineteenth-century café window. This is the central observatory for the whole canal quarter, commanding the swing-bridge, two foot-bridges, the lock, the two quays, and the roads to Bichat and Saint-Louis. Maigret would take up his stand at the counter, watching the bridge through a mirror hanging over the bar.

133 Laverie, 10 rue Bichat, Xme. One of the last hand laundries, a declining trade, the names of customers written on the pink packets containing shirts, vests, pants.

**134   Policewoman, corner of the rue de la Grange-aux-Belles
and the quai de Jemappes, midday, Xme.**
It is late on in the morning and it has become impossible to find any
parking space in the rue de la Grange-aux-Belles. The *agente* has just
turned up, in anticipation of the *sortie des écoles*, to escort across the
busy street small children as they come home for lunch. She will turn
up again at a little before 2 and again at 4–4.15.

135 Patron, Café du Pont-Tournant, rue de la Grange-aux-Belles, Xme.

The *patron*, a Tunisian, at his observatory, overlooking the frontier post of the *pont-tournant* and, like ourselves, watching the day go by, judging the time from the movement in the street. It must now be about 4, as the children are being brought back from the *maternelle*. We saw them on their way to school, at 8 in the morning.

136 La Chope des Singes, quai de Jemappes, Xme.

Next to the *Café du Pont-Tournant*, three in the afternoon, lunch has been served, and this is the sort of small restaurant that will not do dinners. The menu is written in violet ink. The paper cloths have been removed, leaving the flowered wipeable oilcloth.

137 La sortie de la maternelle, 4.15 p.m., corner of the rue de la Grange-aux-Belles and the quai de Jemappes, Xme.

138 Mécanique Générale, 102 quai de Jemappes, Xme.
A workshop as small as those of the XXme, leading off the quay, the upper storey somnolent in the afternoon sunshine, the shutters opening on the ground-floor onto an over-furnished sitting-room.

139 **L'heure de la récréation, school, rue Jean-Poulmarch, Xme.** The sound from behind the wall is like that of a bear-garden. The trio has just climbed over the wall and insists on being photographed.

140 **Quai de Valmy, Xme.** A Senegalese or a Gabonais, checking on the afternoon races at Vincennes, on the banks of the canal.

141   Fumisterie, 6 avenue Richerand, Xme.
Utrillo's Paris, but in the Xme, near the canal, two peeling plane trees, to match the leprous grey stone, yellow shutters and a dark green shop-front, the whole indeed having the appearance of dating back to 1828.

Our collection would have been incomplete in the absence of a *fumiste*, the adopted profession of the revolutionary demagogue, Hébert, in his disguise as *le Père Duchesne*, Parisian people's philosopher and *marchand de fourneaux*, the stove-pipes prominently displayed on the cover of his paper. *Fumiste* has, of course, another sense, and one that would not apply to the artisan.

142 Défense d'afficher, 3 avenue Richerand, Xme.
Sun and shade on the most famous law in France.

143 Café opposite l'Hôpital Saint-Louis, à l'heure de l'apéritif, corner of the avenue Richerand, Xme.
Two nurses and a houseman, Saint-Louis in reflection and peering over the wall, a hospital that has now lost much of its mystery and horror, and so no longer the subject of popular *complaintes*.

144   Tecno, quai de Jemappes, Xme.
The surviving nineteenth-century workshops of the
quayside on the far bank, with encroaching
modern buildings.

145 Café de la Poste, quai de
Jemappes, Xme.

146 Pan de maison, 140 quai de
Jemappes, Xme.

A particularity of Parisian
architecture, especially on the
periphery, along the canal, or as seen
from the *métro aérien*, Nation-Etoile,
is the cut-off house, like the side of an
ice-cream, a natural focus to René
Clair and Carné, the setting for *Le
Jour se lève* and for the crimes of the
night as revealed in the bright light of
morning.

147   Quai de Valmy, Xme.
Another study of concentration, five o'clock in the
evening.

RIGHT
148   141 quai de Valmy, XXme.
A small, anonymous hotel with blank wall facing onto
the sports' ground, a survivor from the mid-
nineteenth century. The ground-floor a newly painted
cream, the upper floors a Parisian leprous.

LEFT

149 **141 quai de Valmy, XXme, the same hotel, from the rear.**

A country hotel, with wooden balconies, such as the one described in Raymond Queneau's *Pierrot mon ami*, 'a quiet room on the first floor, with a balcony looking onto the walled garden of a convent'.

150 **Children in sports ground, quai de Valmy, Xme.**

The P.E. hour at 4 p.m. with a *moniteur*, the *Hôtel du Lot* (plate 151) on the left.

151 **Hôtel du Lot, 6 rue du Terrage, Xme.**

The *Hôtel du Lot*, fading but still perceptible, in mid-nineteenth-century script, a pale reminder of the transformation of the population of Paris as a result of the construction of the north-south railway network, bringing the Massif Central and the Midi within the radius of Paris, and the consequent influx of casual labour, particularly in the building trade, from the Cantal, the Aveyron and the Lot, to the northern and eastern *arrondissements* of Paris. But very much a relic of nineteenth-century social history, for the rooms would now be housing Algerian, Senegalese and Portuguese workmen.

152   Cité Saint-Laurent, 20 rue du Terrage, Xme.
Workshops in the foreground, a charitable
organisation for young people in the middle distance.
Were it not for the cars, this could be a glimpse of
Balzac's Paris.

153   Courtyard, 22 rue du Terrage, Xme.
As rural, in this very central *arrondissement*, one indeed often taken, by
Louis Chevalier and by other specialists of nineteenth-century Paris as
the very centre of the capital, as the many courtyards of the steep
XXme, as it climbs towards Belleville.

154 Woman in café, rue du Terrage, Xme.
Not in fact a friendly gesture from a *Pernod*-ravaged face, accompanied by a flood of insults. The only occasion in fact when the camera was greeted with hostility.

155 Courtyard, 17 rue Eugène Varlin, Xme.
A Senegalese carpenter outside his workshop, below an elaborate iron balcony. A small printer's clanking in the workshop on the right, a patch of bright sunshine, 5 p.m., in the foreground.

156   **8 rue Eugène Varlin, Xme.**
A shop that seems closed for good, though the two upper floors are occupied. At the far end of the courtyard, a *Pension de Famille*, called *Home Fleuri*, and some organisation concerned with Japan and China.

LEFT

157   2 rue Eugène Varlin, Xme.
A nineteenth-century *boulangerie*, its
base modernised in ugly mosaic,
1920s, *Spécialité de Gugelhopf.*

**158   Médailles, passage
Delessert, Xme.**
Men in their 50s or over are drawn to
the windows of the medal shops,
Palais-Royal, *chez Marie Stuart*, or
place Saint-Germain-des-Prés, *chez
Arthus*, to contemplate with envy the
red and green ribbon of the *croix de
guerre*, the blood red of the *Légion
d'honneur*, the bright blue of the
Mérite, the mauve of the *palmes*,
the green of the *Mérite agricole*
(nicknamed *le poireau*), other more
exotic orders, Tunisian, Moroccan,
Indo-Chinese, a rainbow of ribbons
lighting up old age, impending
retirement, quiet shops under the
arcades, interspersed with stamp-
shops and jade. A small industry with
a guaranteed future, conducted from
a two-storeyed factory off the quays,
Décorations françaises et étrangères,
with all the ranks of the *Ordre de
Léopold*, from *Grand Officier* to mere
chevalier, rosettes, collars, sashes,
shop-windows as irresistible to the
adult male as *boulangeries* to the
schoolboy.

159   A La Belote, 7 rue Pierre Dupont, Xme.
An almost perfect small café in dark green, *Porto Castello* as eternally
fixed in the 1920s, as the equally reminiscent *Porto-Flip*, in white
letters, in the *passages*, quartier de la Bourse, quartier Saint-Lazare of
Aragon's *Le Paysan de Paris*. Inside there are only two tables, at one of
which are seated, wearing bérets, four card-players, as if to justify the
title, a little before the evening *heure de l'apéritif*. If Maigret has an
enquiry to make concerning an inhabitant of the quarter, he could
start here, with a *petit vin de Sancerre*.

160   Bouchons, 213 rue du Faubourg Saint-Martin, Xme.

Bouchons in bright yellow, on a dark bottle-green background soothing and very cool, to match the green raffia blinds, and the quiet of a shop smelling of cork and wine.

The *bouchonnier*, at present asleep inside, in the shade, seems to have a taste for his own products, as indicated by the two corked bottles, half-empty, next to the potted plant; his breathing can be heard in the quiet courtyard, off the rue du Faubourg Saint-Martin, once, in the late-eighteenth century, with its twin, rue du Faubourg Saint-Denis, the busiest, most active street of Paris.

161   Rue du Faubourg Saint-Martin, Xme.
Etablissements A. Claverie, Ceintures, Bas Elastiques,
Corsets, with six windows displaying the full range of
artificial limbs in salmon pink, hands, hips, trunks,
surgical corsets, the central temple of the industry and
a display that would have attracted Raymond
Queneau for its luxuriant fantasy. The lower half of
the building painted in *lie de vin,* or the colour of
dried blood.

The full range of goods is displayed on the busy
north-south axis of the rue du Faubourg Saint-
Martin, on the route of conquering armies, French or
Foreign, perhaps a subtle homage to the military
unijambistes and to those who lost other limbs in
the course of nineteenth-century campaigns. But *la
femme forte* is likewise catered for. The side street is
denied that privilege of display. One would be tempted
to think that the two long 1840-style houses, with
their 46 windows (plus that of a lavatory) house those
employed in this great enterprise; *gaines, soutien-
gorges,* and the endless fight against obesity. But the
rooms are more likely to be let out. The windows on
the main street have no doubt witnessed departures of
troops in 1870 and 1914.

162 Bains Lafayette, 198 rue Lafayette, Xme.
A semi-circular setting fitting of the boulevard du
Crime, Faubourg du Temple, under Louis-Philippe,
the bathing establishment of *les Enfants du Paradis,*
the steaming water of the huge bath gradually
reddening with blood. Towels, soap, shampoo
obtainable at the counter on the right, a damp
warmth, the sound of splashing, of running water and
gurgling pipes, the baths are behind the curtained
windows facing onto the courtyard. There are still a
few such establishments on the Right Bank, but those
on the Left have disappeared, an indication of a
significant shift in the social composition of the VIme
and the Vme in particular. The *bains Racine* (VIme) are
no more than a memory, having been replaced by a
pizzeria.

The walls are of peeling yellow stucco, a faded
grandeur shared by such establishments and by small
casinos in Enghien-les-Bains or once-royal palaces in
Balkan capitals. For those with specialised tastes there
exist *bains doubles*, two or three to be had in such
places, little in demand and so offering immediate
access, though the *bains simples* will generally have to
be waited for, especially at week-ends. The best time
to come is between ten and midday.

163 Les Bains Lafayette, 198bis rue Lafayette, Xme.

The bathing hours have recently been reduced, confined to the former Thursday half-day and the week-end, Sunday morning being the most in demand, so that the customer must continue dirty the first half of the week, making full-scale washing concomitant with *endimanchement*. The reward in fact of work. In our case, a suitable terminus to over eleven hours on our feet, in the canal world of the Xme, the light now beginning to fade at about 6.30.

164   The Gare du Nord, seen from the rue Lafayette.
For the English, the Belgian, the Dutch, the North-German, the Scandinavian, the Pole and the Russian, the way in and the way out, a suitable introduction to the Xme, though most will scarcely pause in the *arrondissement*, still, however, forming the largest concentration of Belgians and of inhabitants of the Nord, who favour the lower end of the long, dull rue Lafayette.

5

XVIIIme arrondissement:
quartier de la Goutte-d'Or.

. . . Ce vieil hôtel, crevassé et mal rechampi, s'intitulait
modestement: le *Continental-Hôtel*. Il était habité par des petites
employées de magasins, quelques personnages indéfinissables, mais
destinés à des carrières libérales, deux ou trois filles soumises
suffisamment âgées et de mines paisibles. Le patron, ancien garçon
d'hôtel à Montmartre, était un Auvergnat . . .

PIERRE MAC ORLAN, *La tradition de minuit*, 1930

. . . Une forte odeur de sang le saisit aux narines. Il trouva le
commutateur et donna la lumière. Alors, il aperçut le décor du carnage.
Une mare de sang sur l'oreiller; une cuvette posée sur une chaise
cannée était remplie de sang. Des éclaboussures rouges maculaient le
papier du mur dans la ruelle du lit. Tout cela sentait horriblement
l'odeur fade des abattoirs . . .

PIERRE MAC ORLAN, *La tradition de minuit*, 1930

UNDER a charming poetical name—akin to *la Butte-aux-Cailles*, *la Grange-aux-Belles*, *le Village Suisse*, and other rural relics or bizarreries of Parisian nomenclature, *la Goutte-d'Or* at one time hid a very ugly, very bloody, very alarming reality; it was the killing ground between the French police and the F.L.N. terrorists, as well as between rival factions of Algerians, and, as such, it was impenetrable to the more prudent European thoughout the years of the Algerian War, though, no doubt even then, most of the long-established inhabitants managed to survive and to get on with their normal activities. It is still sometimes described as the *casbah* of Paris, though there must be rather more Algerians living in the wastelands of the XIIIme, rue Nationale and rue du Château-des-Rentiers. It certainly has a very Arab flavour, even in its shops. The frontier leading to the Goutte-d'Or is the wide and sordid boulevard de la Chapelle, darkened down its middle by the arches of the *métro aérien*, the dismal terrain of very loud-mouthed prostitutes and of cheap luggage shops, as it leads towards the pleasure-lands of Pigalle and the Place Blanche. But the Goutte-d'Or itself is off the tourist routes, the Sacré-Coeur, visible from the *casbah*, being more approachable from the rue Lepic. Nor is the quarter entirely colonised, as it were in inverse order, by North Africans. The further one climbs, the more French and petit-bourgeois the quarter becomes. And nothing could be more respectable and more reassuring than the Villa Poissonnière. In the late-eighteenth and early-nineteenth century, Parisian merchants liked to build themselves summer places on the northern heights; and, up steps, some of these have survived, overlooking the *quartier commerçant*. There are almost as many courtyards as in the Xme and the XIVme, with the same mixed but entirely harmonious population. The main surprise is to discover streets, squares, small parks of provincial tranquillity within three minutes of the *métro aérien* and the screaming boulevard de la Chapelle. Perhaps the Goutte-d'Or should be likened to a *casbah*, for it is full of secret places, of green oases and running water, as it is brushed down the cobbled street by a long-limbed Senegalese in municipal uniform and armed with a long, old-fashioned broom, purchasable at any *marchand de couleurs*. There are even spiky and dusty and rather anaemic palms in the small gardens of the *Villa*.

165 Métro aérien, Boulevard de la Chapelle, XVIIIme.

Just as the canal Saint-Martin represents the particularity of the waterside area of the Xme, of *la Grange-aux-Belles*, so rustic and sweet-sounding, with *le pont-tournant* as its visible frontier post; just as the secret *ceinture* and a waterfall of steps characterise up-and-down Belleville, the *métro aérien* is the checkpoint into the once-frightening *la Goutte-d'Or*, as it is approached, beyond the badlands of the boulevard de la Chapelle, by the gently climbing rue de Chartres. Let *Chiffons* then, just visible, be our *entrée en matière* to the XVIIIme.

166 Chiffons, 8 rue de Chartres, XVIIIme.

Chiffons is as good an entry as any. The *chiffonnier*, who has just put down a bottle of *gros rouge*, drunk *au goulot*, at 8 in the morning, is standing in the entry to his shop, green-fronted. His two hand-carts (*diables*) are up-ended in the street. The restaurant is still closed, but the Tunisian *pâtisserie* has already opened its doors. The rag-and-bone man has a third *diable* further up.

167 Boulevard de la Chapelle, XVIIIme.
The dreary, sordid boulevard, with its cheap luggage,
a prostitute already on the beat at 8 in the morning,
and a *Poste de Police* at the inter-section leading to the
Goutte-d'Or, but no hint of the provincial islands of
calm off the main artery, a little to the right.

168   Rue de la Goutte-d'Or, XVIIIme.
The street names the quarter, as it climbs up, in the
early morning light, towards the hideous white
basilica, the tall corner building, many of the raffia
blinds still down, characteristic of those of northern
Paris, as if architects had sought to match the steep
slopes of the site with windows commanding the
whole of central Paris.

169   Corner of the rue de Chartres, XVIIIᵐᵉ.
Select Hôtel, a sure favourite for an establishment
which is anything but and that has seen a variety of
custom, now mainly confined to Algerian immigrant
workers and residents.

170 Tunisian butcher, 19 rue de la Charbonnière, XVIIme.

Le quartier de la Goutte-d'Or is perhaps the principal North-African concentration of Paris, though, as we have seen, there are plenty of Algerians in the XXme; and there are plenty more in the ill-named rue du Château des Rentiers—for it is a street of the very poor—behind the Gare d'Austerlitz, in the XIIIme. In the latter stages of the Algerian War, la Goutte-d'Or was one of the principal fiefs of the F.L.N. and was the scene of daily, and, above all, nightly violence, both between rival Algerian factions—F.L.N. and *messalistes,* and between the Algerians and the police. It is now comparatively peaceful and quite as colourful as its beautiful name would imply. Here then are the ingredients for a *merguez* or a *couscous mouton.*

LEFT BELOW

171 **Alimentation, 23 rue de Chartres, XVIIIme.**
A rich display of fruit and vegetables, combining the products of
the Ile-de-France, the market gardens of Montreuil-sous-Bois,
with those, more exotic, of the Mahgreb. The shop is already
open for business at 8 a.m.

172 **Les Beignets Tunisiens, 34 rue de Chartres, XVIIIme.**
The clothes hanging from the window are a brilliant cluster of
orange-red, purple, acid green, and blue against the yellow shop
front and the beige of the Tunisian doughnuts and cakes, as in a
narrow street in Marseille, where the line will go right across,
like a celebratory *pavoisement*, when the street is sufficiently
narrow, and thus a reminder, in northern Paris, and just off the
windy, draughty, chilly, boulevard de la Chapelle, of the
Mediterranean.

173 **Hotel Meublé, 25 rue de Chartres,
XVIIIme.**

This is a book about thresholds, just as
private history is about thresholds, *le
seuil, pas-de-porte,* the attempt to look
inside, but, in this case, perhaps not too
far, for this threshold is more alarming
than inviting, the dark spot on the thin,
worn piece of carpet could be blood,
though, in fact, it is merely a smear of oil;
and, up a couple of flights, *la chambre du
crime,* blood on floral wallpaper in mauve
and brown, a body distributed in pieces on
a rumpled bed, with brass knobs at each
end, and on the parquet floor, *photo
d'identité judiciaire* from Lyon's *musée du
crime.* But, much more banally, the
temporary or permanent home of a migrant
worker or the work-place of an *horizontale,*
the sheetless bed covered with a washable
and greasy oil-cloth.

174   Epicerie, 44 rue de Chartres, XVIIIme.
The emblem of Islam alongside *Epicerie*, Tunisian, as
well as French fruit and vegetables, competing in
bright and varied colour with more washing, vaguely
seen behind a closed window of the first floor, the
pretty door, Louis-Philippe ironwork, of No. 44,
opening inwards, to the staircase of the single-
storeyed house, in the climbing rue de Chartres.

ABOVE RIGHT

175   Rue de la Goutte-d'Or, XVIIIme.
A small Tunisian boy standing in the sunny window
of a tailor's shop, a jacket, a large photograph of an
ideally handsome male model with abundant hair and
cuffs, and what appears to be a ghostly outline of a
première communiante in a white dress. Perhaps the large
photograph is designed to signal the little boy on his
future way, though he seems quite oblivious to any
such promised destiny.

176 Courtyard, 34 rue de la Goutte-d'Or, XVIIIme.

A deep courtyard off the rue de la Goutte-d'Or, with the workshop of a stone-cutter at the far end (*marbrier et carreleur*), a survival of *sans-culottisme* in twentieth-century Paris, and, on the left, a line of workshops, surmounted by a single storey, an architecture very much to the scale of Eugène Sue and of Louis Chevalier, and among which the cars form a discordant element. In the right foreground a water-tap, a mounting stone, and more washing. Further down, a carpenter.

177 Entry to staircase sur cour, 34 rue de la Goutte d'Or, XVIIIme.

A staircase, off the same courtyard, a threshold much more reassuring than that of the *Hôtel Meublé*, rue de Chartres (plate 173), as the stairs curl upwards. We can hear children's voices coming from the first floor.

178   Entry to the Villa Poissonnière, off 41 rue Polonceau, XVIIIme.

One of the more engaging middle-class particularities of Paris, along with its glass-topped Louis-Philippe *passages*, situated mostly in the central areas of the VIIIme, the IXme and the Xme, are its *villas*, private roads, closed at night by gates at each end, with individual houses, of a variety of extravagant styles — but all more or less *style-Larousse* (see under *Maison*), Second Empire, High-Third Republic, or 1900–20, each house fronted by exotic gardens, and decorated in a variety of arabesques in coloured tiles and slates, with a predominance of pale blues, light yellows, pinks, light beiges and washed-out mauves, on the iron gate or on one of the pillars of each, a flowered *plaque*, with the name of a tree or a flower or a declaration of independence: *Mon Abri*. There are such enclaves in the quartier des Ternes and in the Villa des Peupliers, in the unlikely XIIIme. The Villa Poissonnière descends steeply from the level of the rue Polonceau. Halfway down on the right, there is a *Pensionnat de Jeunes Filles* and a day nursery (paying) for small children. Opposite is a school for oriental dancing, another house advertises a masseuse and a specialist in pedicure, another a private language school that provides lessons in Esperanto. From half-way down, at 9 in the morning, come the awful scratching of a violin and the tinkling sound of someone practising on an ill-tuned piano; and the green and yellow metal sign on a fortified iron gate, alongside a black and white *Chien méchant* and an elaborate iron bell-pull announces *Ecole de Dessin Geneviève Heurteau, diplômée des Arts & Métiers*. Only local dogs are admitted, most of them are poodles or very small creatures; but there are also plenty of cats (one of them on my lap) wearing red or blue collars and little bells. There is more than a hint of lilac dresses, print frocks, dancing shoes, and ladies wearing 1920-type *bandeaux*, who admire Loti, and who try their hand at engraving, water-colours, or poetry. It is hard to think how the tapestry-maker gained a hold in such a middle-class fortress. The Villa is approached at each end through an arch. It might be a quiet street in Saint-Mandé rather than north-east Paris. The enclave seems very remote from the *casbah*, though the latter starts just beyond the bottom archway. But when the Villa was first thought of, there was still no *casbah*.

179 Villa Poissonnière, off the rue Polonceau, XVIIIme.

Top two storeys of a house with garden, half-way down the private walk, on the right, within the Villa, with light blue, pink and green arabesques, as a frieze above the first floor windows, in coloured tiling, suggesting a small casino or a *Pension de Famille* in 1900 French-Primer style, or a private bank, or the home of a retired colonial official, behind a garden planted with palm trees, the ultimate in fact in middle-class domestic architecture, 1900–14. The owner, a lady wearing a flowered pinafore and bedroom slippers, her hair dyed a reddish brown, very polite and well-spoken, explained to us rather carefully, as if accepting us within her conventions:

nous sommes bien tranquilles ici, nous sommes tous voisins, on est entre amis, on ferme les deux issues au cadenas la nuit, as if to suggest an embattled middle-class enclave in an area potentially hostile. She had just lent her watering can to a neighbour. She might have been the widow of an officer or of a colonial official. The *Pension de Famille* opposite, one felt, would be eminently *recommandable*, a place indeed to acquire French without tears. *Maternités*, nursing homes, Turkish baths might be similarly decorated, the name of the house, *Les Tilleuls, Ça me suffit,* surrounded by formal flowers, on a coloured metal *plaque* on one of the pillars of the entry, an electric bell in the metal gate.

180 House at the top of steps, leading off 23 rue Polonceau, XVIIIme.

An eighteenth- or very early nineteenth-century scene, in the bright October sunshine of 8.30 a.m., a handsome house, at the top of a flight of steps, rewarding the climber with the unexpected revelation of its beauty, a walled garden, a tap, plants in stone pots, an uneven *pavé* in brown, beige and light grey, the opening shutters breathing in the clear, motionless day, a scene as much from the Ile-de-France as from northern Paris.

181 Staircase and October sunlight, 33 rue Polonceau, XVIIme.

Better even than a threshold, this both takes us *up* and *inside*, on the level. One can *feel* the grooves of the well-worn stairs, the smoothness of the banister, as it gleams in the sun, and there is a *vue plongeante* towards potted plants and a nightdress hanging from a balcony, as the snakelike and ancient *tuyauterie*— waterpipes and electric wiring, the one gurgling, the other dangerous, crawl in complicated and curling *arabesques*.

182 Enseignes, 23 rue Polonceau, XVIIIme.

The only sign-writer in our collection, but peculiarly combined with *Pressing*, and *Antiquités*, though M. Klein can surely not be engaged in all three activities. Perhaps, like the advertisement for the coiffeur, beautician and wig- and toupet-merchant, they are merely advertisements; for what is going on inside, under the strong lights, is sign-painting, in harmony with the artistic lady in her bower and holding her palette, a Second Empire figure identifying the trade within. M. Klein, in béret, came out to talk to us, commenting, on the subject of the Quarter: *Je suis à peu près le dernier Français à exercer mon métier par ici*, and using an unflattering collective expression to designate his Algerian neighbours. The shop-front is elegant Louis-Philippe.

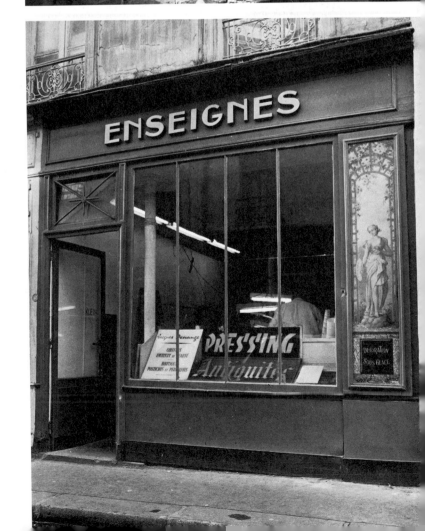

183   Egoutier, rue Polonceau, XVIIme.
A very good-looking Sénégalais, just up from the sewers—he has replaced the heavy cover of the iron ladder leading down—looks at Nicholas quizzically, as he handles an alarming-looking knife. Africans have begun to rejoin the Algerians in the Goutte-d'Or.

184   Boulangerie on the corner, 23 rue Polonceau, XVIIIme.
The finest *boulangeries* are on corners, facing two ways and thus offering a double aspect of *gourmandise* to onlookers covering a wide age-span. Côté-Polonceau, a display of éclairs, *têtes-de-nègre*, *palmiers*, *courriers de Brest* and boxes of baptismal sugared almonds. The bread is inside. The lettering and the coloured windmill under glass are Second Empire; and *boulangeries* are the only shops thus illustrated. The café-restaurant opposite is caught in the obliging mirror, the rue des Gardes in another.

185   17 rue des Gardes, XVIIIme.
Private dwelling-houses from the First Empire, a
period devoted mostly to prestige public building, to
triumphal arches, and to immense barracks, are rather
rare in Paris, so this entrance, surmounted by cherubs
holding an escutcheon and its beautifully proportioned
green *porte-cochère* seemed to qualify, if only for its
impersonality, symbolic of a severely inhuman and
anonymous régime.

INDEX OF STREETS